Shoreham Harbour Insights

250 years at the heart of the community

Shoreham Port 1760–2010

250 YEARS

shoreham port

First published in the UK 2010
by Shoreham Port Authority
Nautilus House
90–100 Albion Street
Southwick
Brighton BN42 4ED

ISBN 978-0-9565781-0-5

Managing Editor: Professor Fred Gray
Text: Adam Trimingham
Picture research: Jackie Marsh-Hobbs
Design: Margot Richardson

Front cover: Shoreham Harbour viewed from the bridge of *MV Hajo*, 2 June 2010.
Photo by William Barker, Deputy Harbour Master

Back cover left: Workmen inside the west pier, 1928. *WRSO*
Back cover right: Cargo ship the *Seaford* entering the lock, early 20th century. *SBIT*

Right: Boat damage to East Pier, late-19th century. *SPA*

Contents

Foreword

There are two Shoreham Harbours in my life – the one that was such a vivid part of my childhood, and the one of today which features so often and so prominently in the life of my alter-ego, Detective Superintendent Roy Grace of Sussex CID.

As a tiny boy I used to beg my dad to take me there. In those days you could drive along the entire quay, and he used to delight in scaring me by swerving the car right up to the murky water's edge. Later I was to discover, to my fascination, the harbour's dark underbelly, the suicides and the murders that took place there and the wider – and for me deeply fascinating – role it played in the criminal history of Brighton.

From the age of eight, when I got my first bike, I used to cycle endlessly around the harbour in my holidays and at weekends. It was a magical, mysterious and romantic place for a small boy with a wild imagination. The warehouses, the gantries, the massive coal bunker of the power station, the cargo ships with their strange flags and even stranger names, the lorries, the sailors and stevedores, the hustle and bustle. More than anything else I can remember its smells – the reek of acrid gases, the smell of coke, coal, timber, paint, varnish, and that heady tang in the air of salt, rust and putrid fish, that seaside landladies used to tout as 'ozone'.

My first experience of death was in this harbour, too, when I was nine. A close friend of my parents, called Frank Ogden – a prominent baker in the town – drowned off a yacht in the harbour mouth after being knocked in the water by the boom, late at night. The image haunted me for years.

As a teenager I kept a sailing dingy at the now long-gone Lighthouse Club (later the scene of a real double murder!) and remember one time capsizing in a squall, just inside the harbour mole, myself and a friend sitting, terrified, on the upturned hull unable to right the boat, as a tanker was coming in straight at us. An unsympathetic Harbour Master yelled at me through a megaphone to get out of the way. 'How?' was all I could yell back at him. I wasn't bold enough to try my luck with: 'Sail before steam!'

Today, in almost all of my Brighton-based Roy Grace novels, Shoreham Harbour features significantly. Whether a dredger docks with a body caught in its drag-head, a van is pulled out of the water with a body inside, a villain imports his contraband, or a serial burglar likes buying his fish here…. Just a tiny reflection on just how key a role this magical place plays in the lives of all of us who live in Sussex.

Peter James

Left: A Lebanese cargo ship moored at the Lay-By wharf opposite the Lady Bee Marina, 1960s. *SPA*

Introduction

By marking any major anniversary in a publication you have to make sure that it is interesting and readable. This is made doubly more difficult if your anniversary is marking the 250th year of your foundation. So much has happened in those 250 years that our compilers are faced with a huge amount of material with the result that editing decisions are more about what to leave out rather than what to put in. We have used many illustrations throughout the book, (many of which have never been seen before) which I hope will make this 250th anniversary publication an interesting and easy read.

As you will see as you read through the pages and look at the many photos a great deal has happened since 1760. This book not only gives a larger than life snapshot of the personalities involved but with it comes murder, smuggling, vicious storms, war, shipwrecks, accidents and ill fated commercial ventures. Somewhat like a novel of our top ten crime writer Peter James who has used Shoreham Port for some of his plots and who generously supplied our foreword.

The port over 250 years has had to change and adapt on numerous occasions to customer demand, public opinion, political policies (both local and national) new technology and new working practices. As you will see this has not always shown itself to be a seamless process – sometimes it has been a bumpy ride!

In this anniversary publication we hope to bring to life the changes over those years, the personalities involved and to lay out the diverse activities of the port during this long period and also to give you a glimpse of what we hope Shoreham Port will be for the future.

A massive thank you must go to Adam Trimingham who researched and wrote the main text, Jackie Marsh-Hobbs who researched and captioned the illustrations, Margot Richardson, the book's designer, and the editor, Professor Fred Gray. Huge thanks also go to the many people who have donated their stories, reminiscences and photos for inclusion in this 250th anniversary publication.

Lastly but by no means least we have to recognise the achievements over the years of our workforce from port managers to our stevedores and thank them for their dedication in building the port so that we can publicly recognise 250 years of achievement. Long may it continue.

Dennis Scard

Dennis Scard,
Chairman, Shoreham Port

Left: The harbour at low tide, close to the entrance. Painting by William Powell, 1928. *PM*

Harbour history

There has been a harbour at Shoreham for more than a thousand years thanks to the River Adur which has a convenient estuary. But the trouble with this river, little known outside Sussex, is that it never could decide exactly where to enter the sea.

Each time there was a storm, the estuary changed. Often it was moved east because of longshore drift from the west so that at one point, it was more than three miles from Shoreham close to what is now Hove Lagoon. Nearby Wish Road gained its odd name from the marsh. Further problems were caused by the formation of a shingle spit and silting up of the river, creating mud islands.

Eventually the great and the good decided to do something about it. So it was that in June 1760, 21 men met at the Star Inn, New Shoreham, as the commissioners of Shoreham harbour. They were local landowners, clergymen, aristocrats, shipbuilders and merchants. Their aim was to make a new cut from the river to the sea so that the port would have a permanent entrance.

Already they had the lesson of Old Shoreham before them. This settlement, near what is now the toll bridge, had been the main port hundreds of years ago but the river had silted up and trade had moved downstream to New Shoreham.

The commissioners drew up plans for an entrance a mile away at Kingston-by-sea with piers on either side and appointed

The Preamble to the Shoreham Harbour Act, 1760, reads as follows:

> Whereas the navigation through the present entrance into the harbour of New Shoreham in the County of Sussex is very dangerous, and improving and maintaining the same will be of great utility to the trade and navigation of this Kingdom ... and it shall be lawful to and for the said Commissioners, or any 11 or more of them, at any time or times, from and after the 1st day of July 1760 to make a new cut through the sea beach, opposite the village called Kingston-by-Sea, about a mile to the eastward of the said town of New Shoreham and to erect a pier or piers and to do such other works as shall be necessary, in order to make and maintain a new and more commodious entrance to the said harbour.

John Reynolds as engineer. They promoted a Bill in Parliament which eliminated some ancient practices.

One of these was that the Lord of New Shoreham claimed anchorage, boomage, and meterage, collected by officers of his court, between the harbour entrance and Old Shoreham ferry. But in spite of the Bill, parishioners claimed in 1766, by what right is unknown, that the vicar and constable were entitled to a bushel of coal, salt, or imported grain from every vessel bringing them into the harbour.

All went well until it came to driving in the piles. Those driven in to their full length of 16 feet survived but lazy workers for

Left: Shoreham Harbour (detail) by Richard Henry Nibbs (1816-1893). An obituary writer argued that 'Nibbs could float a ship on canvas in the style no other artist could match'. *SPA*

The harbour shown on Richard Budgen's map of Sussex, 1724. The entrance to the harbour was remarkably close to the then village of Hove.

There were also problems with thoughtless seamen who chucked their ballast into the harbour. They were threatened with prosecution but the practice continued. The commissioners had their hands full with all these problems and the port was strapped for cash.

Despite that, the commissioners lowered dues on many occasions during the second half of the century in what historian H C Brookfield calls a consistent and courageous policy. They were rewarded by an increase in the value of imports from £1,876 in 1753 to £7,164 in 1805.

In 1789, Caleb Burrows was appointed harbour master and his reports of damage to the harbour were depressing reading. In 1800 he reported that the harbour was in a changeable and uncertain state. Action was needed to stop drift in every sense of the word.

Shoreham people, concerned that the commissioners were being idle, called a meeting of their own and asked the engineer William Jessop to make a survey. He reported that the entrance had moved nearly a mile eastwards since 1760 from the position of the new cut. It was moving at 100 yards a year and he thought it best to let the river find a natural entrance at the Lagoon. There was opposition to this on the grounds that the harbour would then benefit Brighton rather than Shoreham.

In 1810, the engineer John Rennie, who had an international reputation for rail and marine expertise, was called to report on the harbour. He agreed with Jessop that the Lagoon exit was the natural one. The commissioners agreed and were prepared to support a Parliamentary Bill for the work to be done. But once again no action was taken.

Five years later a local captain named William Clegram produced a report that diametrically opposed the views of Jessop and Rennie that the harbour entrance would be wider and deeper in Hove. A friend and colleague of his called William

contractors cut the tops off many of them, did not drive them as deep, and sold the surplus as timber.

The new entrance was a success for two years until the half length piles were undermined and the piers collapsed. Men with horses tried to remove the shingle regularly but the harbour mouth began to move east once more. Local landowners also complained that the new cut had affected their holdings. Dams had to be built to protect land at Southwick and compensation paid.

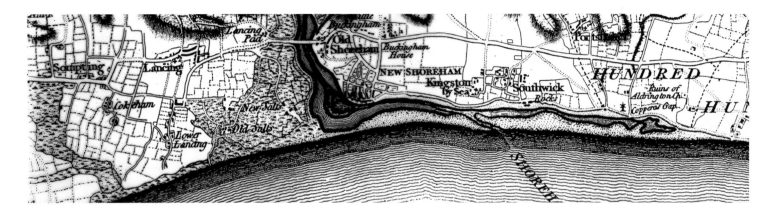

Top left: This 1795 map reveals how the artificial 1760s entrance was unstable and had been moving to the east. Note also the 1781 toll bridge.

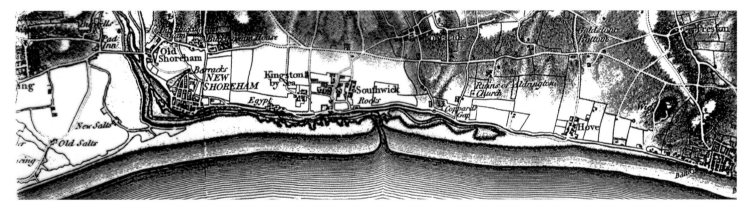

Middle, left: This 1813 map illustrates the continuing eastwards movement of the entrance. The map maker continues a tradition of using the place names Old and New Shoreham. 'Shoreham by Sea' began to be used in 1911. Other place names including Egypt Wharf continue to the present day.

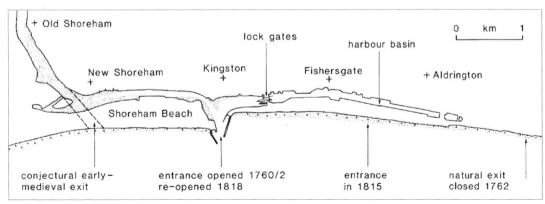

Bottom left: The changing harbour. Note the island – most probably 'Survey Island' – in the river opposite New Shoreham, which was covered by the sea at high water. The easterly drift of shingle and sand, forming banks and bars, was a constant problem and a hazard to shipping. *DR*

Chapman was asked to produce a more detailed report and he came to the conclusion that the original site of the new cut at Kingston was the best. He felt that a deep entrance contained with piers could be built there but on a far more substantial scale than in 1760. He put the cost at £36,432, a large amount for those days.

Chapman gained sustained support for his plans and called expert witnesses to a town meeting at Shoreham before facing the commissioners who approved his report unanimously. Another Bill was prepared and it passed through Parliament in 1816.

The Shoreham Harbour Act said that the local population was increasing and trade would be extended if the port were improved. It added: "It will not only afford great protection to shipping in distress but will also form a commodious station for His Majesty's cruisers in time of war." This was important at a time when Britain had just defeated Napoleon.

To make sure the entrance did not collapse again, the commissioners made sure the piles for the piers were driven down 24 feet and also marked as the property of the port. In addition they authorised protective banks to avoid damage to neighbouring land.

The new cut was opened in 1819 but went well above budget by £22,000, causing more financial worries for the commissioners. But within a few years familiar problems had recurred. The entrance had been damaged by a collision with a brig in 1821 and the formation of a shingle bar. Clegram, in a further report, recommended more work including strengthening groynes. In 1822 he obtained support for this from the eminent engineer Thomas Telford.

Telford backed the locally produced plans for a cut at Kingston and hoped the commissioners would succeed in establishing the harbour on such an exposed stretch of coast.

But the new entrance proved to be a success. More and more ships began to use the harbour with the numbers of vessels rising from 198 in 1817 to 718 in 1823: an increase of over 350 per cent in just six years. From that time on, Shoreham could claim to be a proper port rather than a small harbour constantly at the mercy of storms.

There had been a port on the Adur at least since the Roman period. At this time it was called Portus Adurni and connected to London by a highway. Saxons arrived in the area around 500 AD, giving Shoreham its name. King John landed at Shoreham with a large army in 1199 and made it a royal arsenal.

Frequent orders were given to supply warships to the Navy. For example, in 1346 Shoreham supplied 26 vessels for Edward III to fight the French: the number was more than that supplied by London, Dover, Bristol or Southampton.

Shoreham had sent ships to France, mainly the Normandy coast, at least since the 12th century but they were small and conditions were always uncertain. Details have been kept of imports of wine and exports of other commodities including wool and cloth.

There are few records at all of trade in the 14th and 15th centuries and in the following century, boats were said to be loaded there in an unregulated way. Even Brighton, which did not have a harbour and instead beached boats on the shore at low tide, fared better at this time.

By the 18th century, trade had perked up a bit which is why the commissioners were interested in the new cut. Timber became the main commodity, starting an association with Shoreham which has lasted to this day. Without the new cut, Shoreham would probably have died as a trading harbour against competition from Littlehampton and Newhaven in Sussex. Dover and Southampton on other parts of the south coast provided a more distant threat.

Detail of an impressive oil painting that used to hang in the boardroom of the old port authority building. It is unsigned and undated, but is most likely by Richard Henry Nibbs. It captures a busy harbour entrance with an assortment of vessels maneuvering past the wooden piers, looking out from Kingston beach. Nibbs exhibited seascapes at the Royal Academy between 1841 and 1888. *SPA*

The *Royal Escape*

Shoreham's most famous visitor in the 17th century was the future monarch Charles II who was fleeing from the Roundheads at the time. He travelled to Sussex in 1651 after being defeated in the Civil War at the Battle of Worcester.

Arriving in Brighton with his colleague, Lord Wilmot, he was introduced to Nicolas Tettersell, a local man who owned a small coal brig called the *Surprise*. Tettersell originally charged £60 for two passengers but upped the demand another £200 when he recognised the monarch.

After staying a night in Brighton, Charles and Wilmot arose early and rode to Shoreham where the boat was moored. They were accompanied by Tettersell and a crew of four to Fécamp in Normandy where they arrived the following morning. The King was carried ashore on the shoulders of a crew member called Richard Carver.

Charles returned to England for the Restoration in 1660 and shortly afterwards Tettersell moored the *Surprise* on the Thames near to Whitehall. In July 1660 she was refitted at Deptford dockyards, and then renamed the *Royal Escape* becoming part of the Royal Navy. He made Tettersell a captain in the Navy and later granted him a pension. With the money, Tettersell bought the Old Ship Hotel in Brighton and later became High Constable.

Carver also contacted the King and secured his agreement to pardon hundreds of Quakers and other dissenters in return for saving his life.

Detail of the *Royal Escape* after van de Velde, Nicolas Tettersell's vessel the *Surprise* as refurbished for Charles II. The painting is now in the Sussex Yacht Club.

Locks and docks

Once the harbour entrance had been built, the way was open for Shoreham, then a tiny port serving a local area, to expand. It was the nearest port in England to a long stretch of French coastline, and it was no surprise that passenger services started in 1824, going to several points in Normandy. There was even a service to Dieppe before Newhaven took over this role in 1848. But the harbour proved hard for steamers to enter during rough weather and there were several expensive collisions causing damage to piers.

This, added to general wear and tear, led to further improvements in the 1840s including a lot of extra piling. There was also a brisk trade in coal for Brighton especially with extensive coal yards at Kingston.

But it was the railway that really resulted in a boom at Shoreham. It arrived in 1840 and there was soon a spur from the Brighton to Shoreham line which went right into the harbour. It remained there for more than a century before being removed in the 1960s.

With few canals and navigable small rivers in Sussex, the railway was vital in producing fast and efficient transport to the port, especially when the network expanded to connect with most of the country over the next two decades.

Because the railway was built so early to Shoreham, this gave the port a significant advantage over its East Sussex rival,

Newhaven, which lasted for seven years. The link into the harbour was achieved through a bridge of 31 arches, each one 30 feet wide.

The London, Brighton and South Coast Railway made its own coke at the harbour which was more good news for the commissioners. But the company upset other traders by making an extra charge for using its wharf.

Timber ponds were also constructed at this time, some several hundred yards long, used as a method of seasoning wood. They stretched all the way from Shoreham to Hove.

Far left: 14 February 1933 looking east. Dredging in front of the east entrance of the new lock, in preparation for the opening ceremony in March. *SPA*

Left: A railway line into the port at Kingston, going under the road through a humped bridge to the quays where there were turning tables to assist in manoeuvring locomotives. The railway connection at the wharf was provided to bring in heavy equipment and materials by sea when the railway was being built since at that time there was no connection to London. *SPA*

The first steps were taken to make Shoreham a modern port in 1854-5. The eastern arm of the harbour, the old river bed, was dredged and made into a canal with a lock being built at the Southwick entrance, while the western arm remained subject to tides. This helped encourage the major developers of the port such as the gas and electricity companies, making the harbour much more industrial than it had been.

Other large industrial buildings around the harbour included the chemical works on Shoreham Beach, built in the 1870s to use by-products of the gasworks, the Dolphin soap works, Eversheds at Kingston and Flinn's dye works at Fishersgate.

But it was not all plain sailing for the commissioners who were forced to borrow money for the harbour improvements. They were also involved in three long and complicated legal disputes over land, the responsibility for paying the poor rate and the latest Shoreham Harbour Bill.

The port also looked at a grandiose scheme, once the canal had been opened, for a ship canal from Shoreham through the heart of Sussex to the Thames costing the staggering sum of £4 million. For a debt-ridden authority, it was simply not possible and a link in West Sussex through the Wey and Arun canal was abandoned in 1871.

In 1873 the commissioners were replaced by trustees with greater powers who included several of the old members. And the shift east of the port's focus was symbolised by the building of new offices at Southwick in 1887.

The customs house in Shoreham High Street was superseded in 1880 by one at Kingston, and a coastguard station was built in 1900 to replace the one on Shoreham Beach.

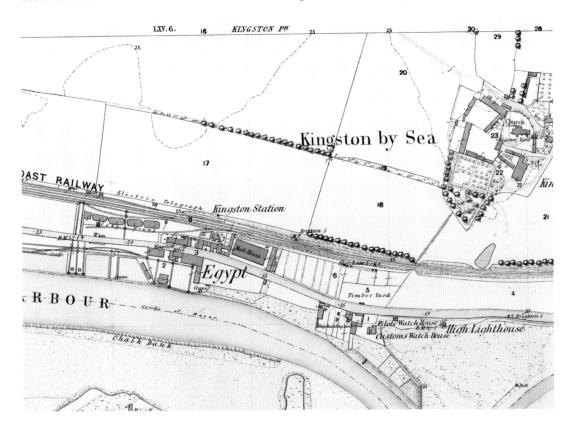

PORTSLADE, SHOWING ELECTRIC LIGHT WORKS

Extensive repairs and renovations were made to the port in the 1870s costing £85,000. They included dredging the harbour and repairing the piers and groynes. The work was carried out by two trustees, Walter Wood and William Ball. They resigned while the work was going on and rejoined later. This was not considered improper, as it would be today, though the work ran into a great many problems.

Judy Middleton, who wrote a history of the harbour's first 120 years, said: "The harbour was run on a shoestring and improvements were haphazard and sometimes disastrous. But by the end of the 19th century, the days of the old gentlemen amateurs were fast running out."

The trustees began to meet monthly instead of quarterly, conducting themselves on a more businesslike footing. With the building of a power station in 1906, the port was booming with huge amounts of coal being brought to Shoreham. Coal was also needed by the gasworks and by the expanding town of Brighton.

But the First World War reduced trade to almost nothing and by the 1920s Shoreham Harbour was a fairly rundown, ramshackle place. There are reports of the trustees dealing with complaints, particularly from the gasworks about the state of harbour roads, and certain reluctance by the worthies to do much about it. They did not have much money and guarded it carefully.

They also considered every minor item, discussing matters that would be left to managers now, such as whether people should be given leave. All the wages were dutifully laid out in neat handwriting in the minute books. No one, not even the general manager, got very much and the unskilled posts were paid very little indeed.

Left: The first electricity generating station, just west of the gasworks, built to keep up with the demand from Brighton and the surrounding area. *MM*

Below: The gasworks, built in the 1870s, were the first major development on the beach side of the canal. *MM*

CANAL SHOWING GAS WORKS, PORTSLADE.

Right: 'Southwick and Fishersgate from Portslade' by James Kinnear, 1879. A paddle tug tows two lighters. Southwick is in the distance and the prominent buildings on the right middle ground are at Copperas Gap, Portslade. *RP&M*

Below: Looking east to a line of cargo ships waiting – perhaps safely aground – in the dredged channel before entering the lock and the security of the canal. *SPA*

They changed the name of the harbour from New Shoreham to Shoreham in 1926 but not much else altered over the years. For a long time after the war, there were 25 trustees, a large number to get round the table. Twelve of them were councillors from five different authorities, six being from Brighton which did not geographically even cover the port. Other trustees included representatives of the port users and the gas and electricity undertakings.

When the trustees were remodelled into the port authority, their numbers were cut to 12 with some councils having to share a representative but a space at the table was always kept for a delegate from organised labour. For many years this was George

Working on the port

Top left: Workmen laying a roadway along the north wharf in Aldrington basin, 1928. *WSRO*

Top right: Repairing the breach to the sea via the south gut, 23 June 1907. *SPA*

Bottom left: 1 May 1931, men working at the Blockyard on the towing path looking east. *SPA*

Bottom right: Marc Wadey and Jordan Wyatt fixing hardwood fenders in the Prince George Lock. Hard hats and fluorescent tops are part of the safety equipment worn by today's port workers. *SPA*

The first lock in the early 1920s separating the dredged channel in the foreground from the more stable waters of the canal. The steam paddle tug *Stella* can be seen just to the west of the lock. The south gut ran between canal and sea and was spanned by the Jubilee Bridge between 1887 and 1920. *ND*

Elphick, formidable district organiser for the transport workers, the biggest union in the land.

Members used to enjoy a good lunch before the meetings, originally held at Brighton Town Hall, but later switched to the port offices. They did not always get on and after one particularly bibulous meal, Labour councillor Maureen Colquhoun from Shoreham pointed at ancient Tory alderman Victor Nicholls from Brighton and asked in a booming voice: 'Who is that fat rude, drunken old man?' Nicholls retaliated by suggesting that

Shoreham Council, which appointed her, should choose someone else so that business was conducted speedily. His Brighton colleague, Stanley Theobald, said members deserved the occasional luncheon after giving service to the port.

Brighton Liberal councillor and yachtswoman Frances Hix (now Lindsay-Hills) was on the authority in the late-1980s and gives a snapshot of what it was like. She said:

'I wanted to be on the port authority as I had built my boat at Shoreham (Graham Barnes yard) and had always taken an interest in the shipping. All councillors took on one or more outside body and I decided that was the one I wanted. I could not understand why the Tories were adamant that I could not have it. They gave it to Frank Masefield Baker. I got awkward and wrote to the Secretary of State, or whoever's gift it was in Parliament, and was given the job. I then found out you got paid! Not a lot but genuine money. The Tories saw it as a grace and favour job.

'We met in a rather splendid board room with an amazing model of the complete harbour set into the middle of the board room table. Meetings were followed by lunch and the chairman dished out a superb sherry called Luncheon Dry. I have often looked for it since but never found it. The chairman retired when I was there and cried at his last meeting.

'A lot of business was very technical for many months as much work had to be done on the movement of shingle. I remember some consultants showing a film about how the sea bed affected the waves and I felt horribly sick. Basically the port authority is a big development company. The land and its buildings are very important.

'I went out a couple of times with a member of the Edlin family who had a company for importing sherry which was kept in great vats at Shoreham. I seem to remember there was rather a lot of seepage. I can also remember the tankers pumping Mateus Rose ashore to be bottled.

'I was also on the port health authority which was very interesting. The Russian boats were amazing with lots of facilities on board as the crew were not allowed to go ashore (I suppose they worried in case they didn't come back). The coal barge I went on was spotless and the Indian captain gave me sherry in his quarters and wanted to know what was playing at the Theatre Royal that week.

'The port health inspector was called Sandy and did a good job. He always looked at the crew's quarters first. If they were clean he reckoned the boat was clean. The main hazard was that every ship you went on plied you with alcohol. How I got down the last gang plank I don't know. I remember once leaving my car at Shoreham and catching the train home.'

Staff tended to stay a long time. There are several reports in the minutes of people working for 40 or even 50 years while Captain A G Stephenson served for 22 years as general manager before retiring in 1968.

He joined the port as harbour master and engineer in 1946 soon after the Second World War. He was appointed general manager in 1955. When he retired in 1968, a board minute noted: 'Largely as a result of his energy and determination, the port has grown to be recognised as one of the leading medium-sized ports in the country.'

Starting at the port in 1955 as a clerk, John Harrison rose to become general manager in 1974 and held the post for ten years before retiring. He saw businesses double during his tenure and supervised a switch from coal to general cargo as the main imports. Mr Harrison was a leading member of the Shoreham Lifeboat and the Shoreham and Southwick Rotary Club.

Bill Dodd, the all-knowing town clerk of Brighton who doubled up as port solicitor, also served the trustees for many years with his son Ian following in his legal footsteps.

Captain Eric Wray, a Trinity House pilot, gave 28 years' service to the port before retiring in 1985, helping to maintain a first class pilotage service.

The western arm of the harbour in June 1973, looking east from Surry boat yard to Egypt Wharf, with a mountain of scrap metal behind the cranes. *JL*

In 1933, the Prince George lock, 240 feet long and 40 feet wide was opened and further deepening of the canal was undertaken, mainly to cope with the power station's needs. The old lock was turned into a dry dock. There was a great crowd as the Prince himself, later the Duke of Kent, performed the opening ceremony and sailed through the lock on the harbour tug *Adur*.

The Prince Philip lock was built nearby in 1957 as part of a £3 million scheme. This was 374 feet long and 57 feet wide with lead in jetties at either end to help the ships negotiate it.

MV Balmoral breaking the ribbon on entering the lock during the opening ceremony for the Prince Philip Lock on 20 May 1958. SPA

This 1957 scheme was designed mainly so that larger colliers could serve the two power stations but it benefited the port as a whole. It included building a complete new entrance about 500 yards further out to sea than the old one.

Two new concrete breakwaters were built, the western one 800 feet long and the eastern one extending 1,200 feet. The old east pier was demolished and replaced with a new structure which helped form a new inner entrance. Spending beaches were provided to reduce the wave action in the harbour and the middle pier was rebuilt further north to give greater manoeuvring space.

A report to the trustees at the time said: 'Beyond question this scheme transcends in magnitude and importance anything previously attempted in the history of the undertaking.'

Just after this good news for the port in 1957 came a disaster. Part of the north canal wall collapsed in Southwick, affecting traffic on the main A259 coast road. The road was completely closed for three months and badly disrupted for three years after that. The bank continued to slip for a long time despite efforts to stabilise it. Traffic had to be diverted via Southwick Green where the roads could not take the strain and a gas main had to be rebuilt away from the slip.

The port was criticised heavily, particularly by Southwick Labour councillor Jim Marsh, for being secretive, but issued a statement saying it had to hold back some information in case it was challenged for compensation, which duly occurred. West Sussex County Council took legal action against the port with the gas board and the sewage authority not far behind. It took 12 years to settle, just before the High Court was due to give a ruling in 1969, with contractors used by the port coming off worst.

Although details of the settlement were not divulged, it was widely thought locally one cause had been dredging of the canal to make it deeper so that larger ships could serve the new power

Maintaining the entrance

Top left: Timber piers at the harbour mouth with dredger and tug hard at work keeping the entrance clear. *SPA*

Top right: Working on new timbers, inside the west pier, 1928. *WSRO*

Bottom left: The west pier being rebuilt in 1928. Since the construction of the piers in 1816, *Teredo navalis* worms had eaten almost half of the 18 inch timbers. For the renewed structure, Greenheart and Jarrah timbers were used, with a concrete core inside the new piers. The work on both piers took five years and cost £40,000. *WSRO*

Bottom right: East pier demolition in progress near the northern end, 19 October 1956. *SPA*

The splendid new lock, built at a cost of £100,000, was named after and opened by Prince George. This Dixon Scott photograph shows the tug *Adur II* entering the new lock, possibly before the opening ceremony, as the site has not been cleared of building materials. The celebrations took place on 15 March 1933. Prince George opened the lock aboard the *Adur II*, before going on to launch a new lifeboat and open the lifeboat house. *TNA*

Shoreham prospered by being too small to be nationalised but its size could also be a handicap. There was little space for container ships although some services were started in the 1970s and roll on, roll off services also had a fraught history at this time. A turning basin was created near the old gasworks site in 1977 so that large ships could turn round in the eastern end of the canal.

Top left: *Adur* was one of the last steam-powered bucket dredgers in operation in the 1970s, built in Holland for the Shoreham Port Authority. Here it is alongside a split hopper barge. *SPA*

Left: In 1973 the Shoreham Port Authority purchased land, which enabled work on the diversion of the road and the excavation of the turning basin at the eastern end of the canal. *SPA*

station. Certainly improvement work at the port caused another problem which arose at the same time. Widening the harbour entrance meant that larger waves were experienced on Kingston Beach. On several occasions, autumn and winter gales breached the sea defences and threatened houses in Brighton Road. This resulted in more criticism for the port and expensive new defences to stop it happening again.

The port authority had a policy of property acquisitions in the post war period, which paid off to the extent that in bad trading years it eventually received more money in rents than in harbour dues. It built up an impressive portfolio of land and buildings ranging from the Lady Bee Marina to the former power sites.

A new port authority replaced the trustees in 1968, with further changes following another revision order in 2004.

Below: Cargo ship *Arklow Sea* manoeuvring in the original turning basin midway along the canal, October 2009. *FG*

Securing the locks

Above: Ninety feet of solid masonry weighing 200 tons collapsed from the lock wall in April 1907. *SPA*

Top right: 3 October 1933, the old lock floor looking west. It opened the following September as a dry dock. *SPA*

Bottom right: Prince George Lock, November 1932, looking east before flooding. *SPA*

The first lock had taken five years to excavate and two years to ensure it retained water before it opened in 1855. It made the *London Illustrated News* in April 1907 when the north wall collapsed. In November of the same year, while repairs were taking place, a steam crane fell into the lock taking part of the south wall with it. There were relentless problem with leaking walls and lock gates for the first part of the twentieth century. After the building of Prince George Lock the old lock underwent repairs and was turned into the dry dock. In the early 1990s modern sector-style lock gates were fitted to the Prince George Lock allowing more efficient operation of the lock for smaller boats.

Great national events affected the port. Coal reserves fell low during the miners' strike in the 1920s, which was followed by the General Strike in 1926. In 1984, no coal at all was delivered for seven months during the long strike by miners over pit closures and the port was picketed. There was outrage among unionists when a collier called the *Kindrence* made three deliveries late in 1984. Some of them occupied cranes as a protest but were left stranded there by the port. The seamen's strike of 1966 also affected trade.

Natural disasters also caused problems. There are frequent references in the reports to damaged piers and eroded beaches through gales. But the port did well during the 1987 great gale in which Shoreham recorded the highest gust of wind anywhere at more than 100 mph. Damage cost less than £40,000 and only a few small boats in the Adur capsized. Luckily the worst of the storm coincided with a low tide.

The Mackley family has had a close connection with Shoreham Harbour ever since 1923 when the founder, John Mackley, helped demolish one of the Mystery Towers, built during the First World War.

Next he designed Turberville Wharf with fuel tanks at the port although the scheme was later modified. He went on to design and build more wharves at Shoreham and the firm prospered, becoming a limited company in 1931.

During the Second World War, he invented a timber boom that would have been sunk at the harbour mouth to prevent an invasion by sea. Mackley also built a hinged bridge over the canal at Southwick in 1942.

Originally based at Shoreham, the firm moved to Small Dole south of Henfield in 1955. Mackley undertook work in many different parts of the country but still maintained a connection with Shoreham, making wharves bigger and better. It also undertook work for the power stations and the gasworks. Often

Mackley was called in to undertake emergency repairs. The company also built a pioneering sewage outfall made of plastic in the 1960s and at the same time constructed modern silos.

In 1907, officials at the port tried to regulate the water level in the canal. They only succeeded in draining it of all the water, necessitating expensive repairs. Today large quantities of water are pumped daily into the canal to keep it deep enough.

There have been many emergencies over the years at Shoreham Harbour. In 1876 high winds brought seawater over the beach and into the canal, swamping it. There was a serious fire at Sussex Wharf in 1989 causing damage estimated at £3.5 million, wrecking a crane and a motor cruiser. Another fire in 1992 started in waste paper being loaded on to the cargo ship *Bettina*. It then spread to stacks of timber and almost reached a chemical factory.

In 1981, hundreds of people in Shoreham had to be evacuated when the freighter *Frisian Star* arrived in the port with

A road petrol tanker at Turberville Wharf, looking west to the harbour entrance. Dismantling the remaining Mystery Tower took nine months and was completed in 1924. *SBIT*

Right: A road fuel tanker waiting at the low density fuel wharf, which was situated on the south side of the canal. *SPA*

a leaking drum of a highly deadly chemical called toluene. Nine tons of liquid nitrogen was pumped into the hold to neutralise the risk of explosions. An earlier leak of 20,000 gallons of fuel from the Texaco depot caused concern in 1975 and there was a leak of 400,000 litres of oil from a container in Brighton Road, Shoreham, in 1998.

The death of 24-year-old Simon Jones in 1998 made national news. He was killed only hours after starting work by a crane grab while working aboard the *Cambrook*, a Bahamian registered ship with a Polish crew, on a private berth (not controlled by the port authority). Friends and supporters said that Jones, a student, should have received proper training from his employers, Euromin. In 2001 the company was fined £50,000 for breaching health and safety regulations.

But for a medium-sized port with a long history, Shoreham has generally had a good accident record with few deaths or injuries.

Below: Agrregate dredger *MV Sand Heron* in 1995 illuminating the night. *SPA*

The port has also had its dark side. In 1973 a body was found in the harbour, weighed down. A Dutch ship turned round in the canal and brought it to the surface. It proved to be that of 16-year-old Clive Olive, a Hell's Angel known as Ollie, who had lived in Hove.

The dark side

Two men and a woman were later charged with murder, the prosecution alleging that Ollie's death was revenge for the rape of a woman friend of the accused. The men were convicted and given life sentences while the woman was convicted of manslaughter but later released from jail after winning an appeal. Detective Superintendent Jim Marshall and his team solved the case. He called it one of the most bizarre he had ever encountered and later wrote a book about it.

Before the new road south of the canal was built, the road went right next to the water in two places and many cars failed to make it round the right angle bends. Most of the drivers survived but the cars were invariably write offs. The harbour was also sometimes used as a dumping ground by criminals and in 1995 police found five safes there.

Above: Diving unit aboard the *Phoenix* inspecting the dry dock gates. Alan Poole left, diver Carl Aichroth, Don Butcher and Les Smith far right. *KW*

Left: Men from the diving unit watch from the *Phoenix* as one of the many vehicles they have recovered is hoisted from the Outer Lay-By berth. *KW*

Ships and shipbuilding

For many centuries, Shoreham was a centre for shipbuilding facilitated by easy supplies of timber at one of the most prominent ports in Sussex.

There are records of galleys being repaired for the king at Shoreham in 1210 and 1212 while in 1231 local carpenters were needed at Portsmouth to repair the king's great ship. The Sussex port became one of the most important centres for shipbuilding during this century.

Ships continued to be built there in the 13th and 14th centuries and probably continued over the next two centuries even though there is no surviving evidence of it. In an early 17th century revival, Shoreham became the chief centre in Sussex for shipbuilding with East Indiamen being built there. Sixteen ships were constructed between 1625 and 1636, averaging more than 200 tons.

There were the usual problems with shallow water in the harbour entrance. When the warship *Dover* was launched in 1654 she could hardly get out of the port. This problem caused the building of naval ships to be switched to other ports for a while.

But the industry bounced back with a bang in the late 17th and early 18th century when most of the men-of-war built in Sussex came from Shoreham. Local shipbuilders were famous for the neatness and good sailing qualities of their craft.

The timber was cheap because it was floated down the River Adur from Wealden woods. In 1732 up to 15 merchant ships were built, while in 1766 it was said that shipbuilding was the occupation for most people. Several warships were built, and in 1782 there were still two shipyards.

There was another decline towards the end of the century with silting up again a problem. But some shipbuilding continued, particularly by Edwards and Balley in New Shoreham and May and Thwaites at Kingston who both constructed ships of up to 500 tons.

Far left: The John Shuttleworth yard was taken over by Courtney and Birkett in the 1890s. Situated next to the dry dock on the site of today's Lady Bee, the yard traded until 1938. *ND*

Below: Stows yard surrounded by a wooden fence with a barque on slip next to the ferry hard in the 1890s. *JGC*

The second page of Will Poole's letter describing the repair work to the *Jersey*. The letter starts 'I never saw any ship in such a condition under water since I knew the sea'. It is dated 1670 and believed to have been copied out for R H Penney. *WSRO*

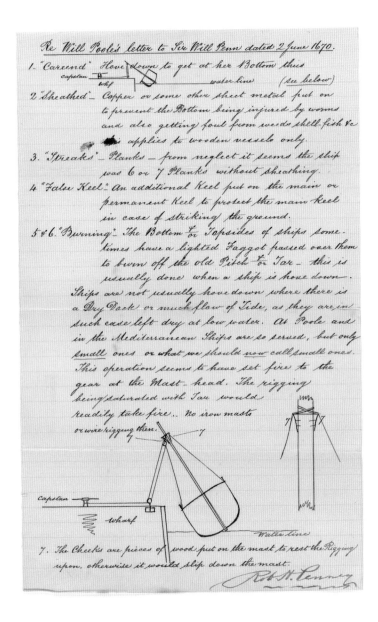

Henry Cheal, the Shoreham historian, wrote: 'For many years the name of Balley, as a builder of ships, was celebrated far and wide.' The vessels were both handsome and seaworthy.

James Balley, according to maritime professional Kenneth Wilcox, was a self made man of local importance. He diversified in 1821 by supervising the piling of the Chain Pier in Brighton. In 1838 he established the Swiss Gardens pleasure grounds in Shoreham, which sometime attracted 3,000, people a day, bringing prosperity to the town.

Smuggling was practised at Shoreham for several centuries with the low-lying coast being favoured for landing contraband. Cheal says the old Sussex Pad pub, with its commodious cellars, was often used as a store.

The increase in population in the 1850s was partly due to a boom in shipbuilding, which employed over 100 people, and Shoreham was noted for the speed of its ships. In the 1860s, John Shuttleworth had a shipyard on the canalised eastern arm of the harbour at Southwick, and William May had the Old Shipyard at Shoreham, each building ships of up to 500 tons.

David Harries in Maritime Sussex says that his firm, May and Thwaites, built small boats at Brighton before moving to Shoreham in 1838 and building more than 50 ships there until 1871.

By that time, the industry was confined to barges and coasting vessels. The sailing ships *Mizpah* (539 tons), *Britannia* (464 tons), and *Osman Pacha* (509 tons), built in the 1870s by William Dyer, were the last large ships from Shoreham. The yards, all minor concerns, never made the conversion from wood to iron.

But small ships continued to be built until the end of the 19th century by men such as Thomas Stow. The yacht builders Courtney and Birkett carried on until the Second World War. Shuttleworth's yard at Southwick, where the Lady Bee Marina is now, continued into the 1970s.

The Old Shipyard, after a brief period as a car factory, was used to build yachts and boats until the Second World War by Francis Suter, a firm that continued, in different premises, in the 1970s. A firm building boats for the navy was established on Shoreham Beach from the Second World War until the 1950s. For a brief period after the First World War, concrete barges weighing about 1,000 tons each were built there.

Cheal says: 'It was always a gala day in the town when a ship was launched. After the official ceremony, involving a bottle of wine being smashed against the new vessel watched by a large crowd, there would usually be a lunch followed often by a ball at the Swiss Gardens.'

In later years as shipbuilding declined at Shoreham, many vessels using the port were built elsewhere, particularly in the north east. One built at Southwick in Tyneside rather than Southwick in Sussex, was the *Portslade*, launched in 1888.

Weighing 594 tons, she had long service as a collier, not being broken up until 1934.

A second *Portslade* was launched in 1936 and was a little bigger but sadly only lasted four years. She was bombed in the Channel during the Second World War off Dungeness. The third *Portslade* replaced her but was wrecked off Dunkirk in the 1950s while the final one was launched in 1955. Built on Wearside and weighing 1,797 tons, she was renamed the *Sassa* in 1977 and broken up eight years later. All of them carried coal to the power stations and gasworks.

Another well-known ship at Shoreham for many years was the paddle tug *Stella*, built for R H Penney at South Shields in 1879. She was sold to the harbour trustees and remained their principal tug for almost half a century until she needed replacing.

Left: A concrete ship being broken up. These 'creteships' were built at Shoreham – with its skilled shipbuilders – after the First World War because of the shortage of steel. *MM*

Below: The launch of *Cretegaff*, one of the creteships. Twenty-one firms around the country received contracts to build a fleet of ships made from ferro-concrete. *ND*

PHOTO. RIPLEY. SOUTHWICK LAUNCHING OF THE CRETEGAFF. LEAVING THE SLIPS

Robert Horne Penney was the son of a ship owner in Poole and the cousin of Southwick ship owner Edward Lucas. He arrived on the Sussex coast in 1852 having already become a partner in a Hampshire firm making sailcloth and rope.

Penney, a Quaker, married Lucy Lucas, daughter of Edward, also Quakers. They had eight children but only three lived to be adults. When Lucas moved to Hertfordshire, Penney took over his business, using a wharf at the end of Grange Road. He also dealt in insurance, sailcloth, coal and corn.

The first ship Penney had built was a brig called *Blue Bell* in 1854. He had another nine built locally in the 1860s, several at Shuttleworth's which is now the Lady Bee Marina.

Later Penney had eight larger iron barques built at Sunderland. The biggest of these was the *Alastor* which weighed 873 tons. They were able to travel round the world. He subsequently moved on to steam ships, with those vessels also built in the North East. Penney also became one of the original Shoreham Harbour trustees in 1873.

The firm's ships travelled worldwide – to Australia, New Zealand, North and South America. Life was hard and dangerous at sea but Penney's ships were strong and reliable.

His son, Robert Alfred, joined the firm in the 1890s and enjoyed a long spell as chairman of the trustees. In 1934 he opened the Prince George lock at Southwick. R H Penney's grandson, George also joined the firm and again chaired the harbour trustees.

George Penney was also a magistrate, treasurer of the Southwick Community Association and a member of West Sussex County Council and Southwick Urban District Council. He chaired the Portslade and Southwick Sewage Outfall Board.

George moved the firm from dealing in commodities such as coal to being largely a ships' brokers. He retired in 1972 and

Penney's Wharf at the harbour was sold. The firm continued in a small way until 1992 after having been a major influence on the port for over a century.

At least one emigration ship left Shoreham in the 18th century, the brig *Enterprise* that sailed for Canada in the spring of 1832. She carried 31 men, 25 women and 43 children.

Shoreham generally has had a good seafaring record but inevitably there have been some losses. One of the worst was the *Britannia*, which left the port in 1883. She ran aground at Sable Island off Nova Scotia in Canada and the entire crew of 13 men perished.

The 1957 improvements enabled much bigger vessels to enter the port. One of the largest ever was the *Nordwoge*, weighing 7,935 tonnes, which arrived in 1977.

Two of the most spectacular ships at Shoreham, even without their sails, were the *Malcolm Miller* and *Sir Winston Churchill*. The masts of these tall ships could be seen for a long way when they entered dry dock for refits in the winter. They are now being replaced by Sail Training Association vessels.

Left: Barque *Britannia* being built at Dyer's shipyard, the Old Ship Yard Shoreham in 1877. Just six years later she was tragically shipwrecked. The shipyard site is now the location of The Bridge hotel. *MM*

Below: First docking of barque *Kaskalot* in 1996 for maintenance in the dry dock. She featured in many films including *The Three Musketeers* and *Cutthroat Island*. *SPA*

The perils of the sea

Top left: The wreck of *SS Brussels* caught on a shingle bar near the entrance of the harbour, 5 July 1922. *SPA*

Top right: Norwegian brig *Hanson* aground by Penney's Wharf in 1915. *SPA*

Bottom left: On 13 February 1914 the *Midown* was wrecked in a storm with the loss of all the crew. Captain Jones was rescued. *MM*

Bottom right: *Athina B* on Brighton beach in January 1980. *SPA*

THE STEAMER MIDOWN FOUNDERED OFF SHOREHAM, FEB. 13TH 1914.

Wooden paddle steam tug *Mistletoe* is believed to have started working at the harbour in the 1870s. Various photographs survive of the steam tug. The *Mistletoe* worked alongside the larger tug *Stella* for 20 years, on occasion helping vessels in trouble. In 1900 the *Mistletoe* was caught in a storm at sea. The skipper, Captain Brazier, was lost and the wreckage of the tug washed up on the beach east of the harbour entrance. *SPA*

Trade

Timber has always been a major import at Shoreham even though Sussex is one of the most wooded counties in England. There are records of its importance going right back to the 18th century.

In those days, timber merchants often stored their logs either in the River Adur or in special ponds nearby. This was so that wood could become seasoned and it was thought that timber used for the masts of ships or scaffolding poles retained its springiness by being kept wet.

Later most of it was stored in covered sheds with layers created so that air could circulate around the logs. But oak for shipbuilding was stored in the open air so that it could be seasoned, sometimes for more than ten years.

Most of the timber came from the Baltic states or from Scandinavia and wood is still a major import today. The only long interruption to trade occurred during the Second World War when the harbour was taken over by the military.

Coal became dominant at Shoreham once the two electricity power stations and the gasworks had been built but it did not have to make such a long journey. Most of it arrived by ship from the mines in north east England

The gasworks alone, at its peak, needed 160,000 tons a year and the total amount of coal imported in 1952 was almost 720,000 tons. The loss of this trade in the 1970s and 1980s was a big blow for Shoreham.

There had been a trade in coal for centuries but Shoreham had a notable rival then in Brighton even though there was no natural harbour there. But the beach was more sheltered than it is today because of the spit by the harbour entrance near Hove. In the 18th century, Brighton imported more coal than Shoreham but lost ground once the Shoreham harbour entrance had been stabilised.

Petroleum might be thought of as a modern import but it has been a feature for more than a century. Its importance increased over the years with the inexorable rise of motoring. One of the major firms was Esso, which had a distribution plant at

THE CANAL PORTSLADE (LOOKING WEST) SHOWING ELECTRIC POWER STATION (56)

Far left: One of the port's Senebogen cranes unloading timber at Outer Lay-By Wharf. It can lift 30 tonnes and cost over a million pounds. *SPA*

Left: A timber pond in the foreground where wood was seasoned and stored. These ponds were restricted to the north side of the canal. *SBIT*

There was a big trade in corn from all Sussex ports in the 18th and early 19th centuries, both in imports and exports. Shoreham is recorded as importing oats in 1788 from France but exported wheat and barley for many years. Eventually as the population increased, wheat was imported. Shoreham also imported eggs, fruit and butter from France.

Ice was also brought into Shoreham from cold countries in the days before refrigeration. It was stored in special wells off Wellington Road in Portslade. Salt, butter and cheese were also imported in the 19th century. More recent foodstuffs imported have included cocoa beans from Africa and at one time Shoreham brought in a fifth of the whole country's needs.

Exports have never been on the same scale but have still been substantial. A century ago the main trade was in Portland cement from the works at Upper Beeding. It was put in barges which were then floated down the River Adur to the port. Now there is a flourishing trade in cereals and metal.

Above: Sailing vessels and the steam paddle tug *Mistletoe* moored next to Albion Street, 12 October 1890. *JGC*

Right: Inside Harvey's, the Bristol based wine merchants, storage shed in the 1960s. *SPA*

Shoreham for 50 years until 1984. Shell was also there, while Texaco continues to use the port to this day.

There is also a substantial trade in aggregates. Cars have been imported through Shoreham and stored on site until sold. Steel is a business growing in importance.

Shoreham was also well placed to import wine from European countries such as France and Spain. Trade was limited until the 1960s when British people developed a fondness for wine which has continued unabated.

At first, wine was delivered rather like oil in bulk with bottling taking place in this country but later, as most tastes became more refined, it was brought in already bottled. Sherry was also imported in casks, particularly for the famous firm of Harvey.

There was a regular steam packet service between Shoreham, Le Havre, Dieppe and the Channel Islands from 1835 until about 1880.

A O Muggeridge was well known in Southwick for many years as a ships' chandlers and a coal and timber merchant. The firm, based in Albion Street, started in 1855 and was immediately successful.

Albert Oliver, grandson of the founder, took it over in the 1920s and during his time the firm was at its peak. It had extensive sawmills and large stocks of coal.

Southwick historian Ted Heasman remembers Muggeridge as a big man who always wore a leather apron and a flat cap. The yard and extensive buildings were full of treasures including wood, hardware and a large anchor.

The Muggeridge family sold the business in 1950. Then the firm established its headquarters at Albion Wharf, moving nearby to Albion Street after acquiring a ships' chandlery there.

It finished in Brighton Road, Shoreham before being wound up in 2007 after 150 years in business.

Left: Ice being unloaded on to a cart in September 1890. If stored in an ice house it could remain frozen for a year. *JGC*

Below: Two mobile cranes working cargo at the Inner Lay-By Wharf in the 1960s. Brighton B power station is in the background. *SPA*

Right: A hovercraft being lifted on to a cargo ship at Inner Lay-By Wharf for export. The 1965 SRN 6 hovercraft could carry 38 passengers. *SPA*

Below: Scrap metal being loaded at Shoreham, bound for Tilbury and then on to China in larger ships. *SPA*

Trade was on a surprisingly small scale before the Second World War and a look at aerial views of the harbour shows how many empty spaces there were. Author S P B Mais, who lived by Southwick Green in the 1930s, waxed lyrical in his book Sussex about how many birds and wild flowers he could see on mud flats by the canal.

But expansion occurred quickly in the 1940s and 1950s. Reports to the trustees, although couched in stilted language, recorded with pleasure how the port was booming. A feature on Shoreham in the Sussex County Magazine noted admiringly that the million ton merchandise figure had been reached for the first time in 1952.

The 1957 lock building allowed large vessels to use the canal, especially colliers serving the power stations. Coal accounted for 60 per cent of the trade at that time but far-sighted managers such as Captain Peter Leighton saw the need to diversify so that Shoreham was not over reliant on one commodity. This was just as well seeing that the power stations and gasworks closed in the 1970s and 1980s.

By 1969, oil was more important as an import than coal while Shoreham's timber trade expanded quickly over these years. The three million ton mark for trade was reached in 1970 and exceeded in 1972 despite a decline by then in coal. Slumps in the 1970s, 1980s and 1990s affected trade badly but the port was able to withstand them and bounce back quickly as the national economy improved.

Shoreham Port hit the headlines in 1995 when there was a series of large demonstrations, lasting for four months, against the trade in live animal exports.

Overall, Shoreham is the busiest port on the south coast between Dover and Southampton. At its peak it has handled more than three million tonnes of cargo a year and it still deals with the best part of two million tonnes, no mean achievement after losing the lucrative trade in coal.

Trading ships

Top: Topsail schooner unloading timber in 1920. The sight became increasingly rare as sail gave way to other forms of powering ships. *JGC*

Above: *John Crafton* was one of the Stevenson Clark fleet, which transported coal and cargo. *SPA*

Above: A sailing barge at a jetty with waiting horse and cart. The Star laundry is on the left and the large building in the centre is the old Britannia flour mill at the south end of Church Road. *SPA*

Left: *Patrai* delivering beech wood from the Black Sea, 4 May 1962. *SPA*

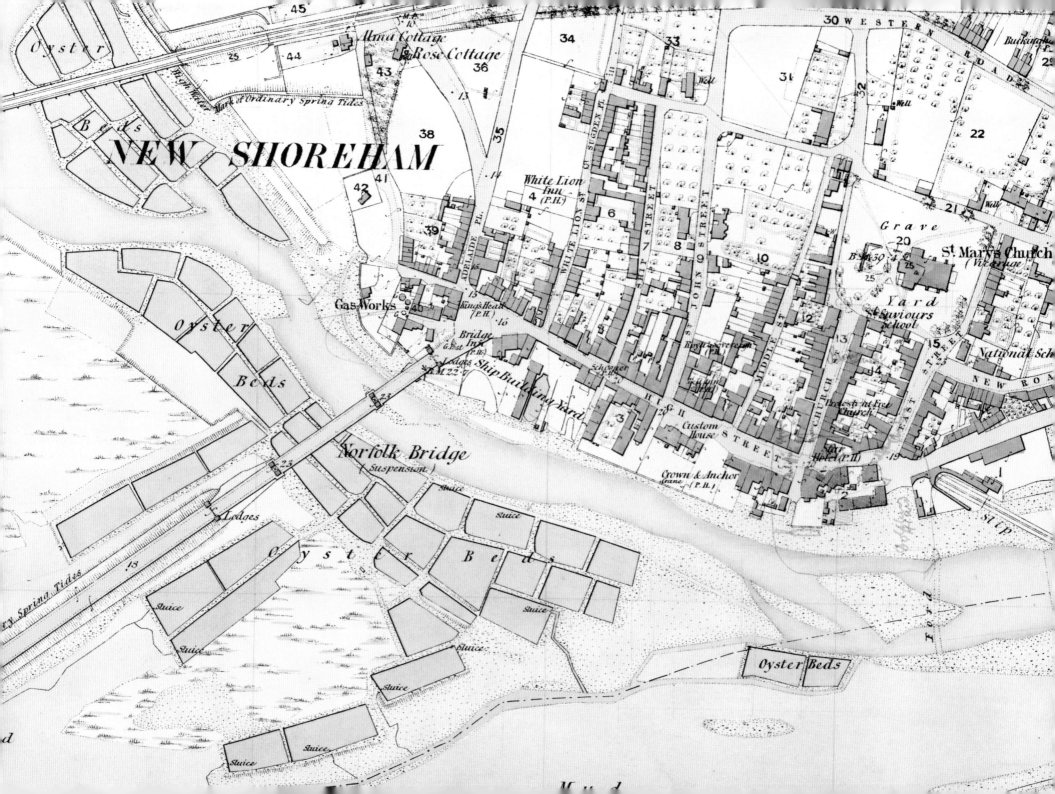

NEW SHOREHAM

Oyster Beds

Oyster Beds

WESTERN ROAD

45

34

33

30

Alma Cottage

Rose Cottage 36

44

43

25

13

35

38

14

White Lion Inn (P.H.) 4

6

7

8

10

St. Mary's Church (Vicarage)

41

42

39

ADELAIDE PL.

WHITE LION ST.

SUGDEN PL.

SHIP STREET

ST. JOHN STREET

MIDDLE ST.

20

25

Grave Yard

22

21

15

Gas Works

King's Head (P.H.) 15

Bridge Inn (P.H.)

Lodges

Ship Building Yard

3

Schooner P.H.

Royal Sovereign (P.H.)

Ship H.

St. Saviours School

National Sch.

NEW ROAD

CHURCH STREET

HIGH STREET

EAST STREET

Norfolk Bridge (Suspension.)

23

23

Ledges

Lodges

Sluice

Sluice

Custom House

Crown & Anchor (P.H.)

Hotel (P.H.)

Oyster Beds

Sluice

Sluice

Sluice

Sluice

Sluice

Sluice

Sluice

Oyster Beds

Mark of Ordinary Spring Tides

Spring Tides

Fishing

Fishing is one of the oldest industries in Shoreham and one that is still flourishing today with many boats moored in the port.

It was first mentioned in 1223 when Hugh Baldefard exported two shiploads of herring and in 1227 boats from Shoreham fished Irish waters. Half a century later the Lord of the Borough claimed an exclusive fishery from Beachy Head to the Isle of Wight for his sailors. Fishermen went as far away as the east coast to collect herring.

Records show that in 1270 a thousand of these fish were paid for a house in the town. It is known that the Shoreham fleet had been away from port for more than four weeks early in June 1311, causing some concern at home. A tax to improve coastal defences against French invasion in 1385 was levied on catches of fish at various places along the coast, including Shoreham, Kingston and Southwick.

For centuries the industry had its ups and downs. Although there was 'good fishing' off New Shoreham in 1595, 14 years earlier only four fishing boats were recorded there, the same number as at Arundel and notably fewer than the 30 at Brighton. In the 1620s fishing at Shoreham was 'decayed' and impeded by enemy action and in the 1670s only three fishermen were recorded. There was a minor revival in the early 18th century but the tonnage declined from 900 in 1709 to 180 in 1757 although neighbouring Brighton may have been included in this.

Oyster fishing at Shoreham was recorded by 1622 and there was an extensive oyster bed opposite the harbour in 1826, supplying the Brighton and London markets. The increasing population in the 1850s was in part attributed to the discovery of further beds. The railway, opened in 1840, provided an easier way to send oysters to London, and grounds further into the English Channel were fished. Oysters were kept in ponds at the harbour until required by the markets, which included some in France.

Almost 100 Shoreham boats were involved in the oyster fishery, and in the 1850s up to 20,000 tons of oysters were sent by rail from Shoreham each year. In the late 1850s there were 60 oyster beds in the Adur estuary and the Duke of Norfolk successfully claimed a right to them. In 1871 the increase in Southwick's population was partly because of new houses for oyster dredgers.

At that time, the Shoreham fishermen wanted to dredge in May despite a ban imposed between that month and the end of August. They maintained that Channel oysters do not spawn until June. But commissioners turned down their plea and when they tried to break the ban coastguards seized their oysters, which were then dumped overboard.

As oyster beds further and further from the harbour were exploited, the boats needed to be larger rising from 20 to 27

Far left: The extent of the oyster beds revealed on a 1875 OS map. The disused wooden frames could still be seen at low tide in the 1930s. WSOR

Right: A row of fishing boats moored in Aldrington Basin, early 20th century. *SBIT*

tons in the 1860s. But the use of steam boats from other ports together with a decline in demand caused a falling off in Shoreham's oyster fishery. By 1905 Shoreham and Southwick had only one oyster merchant each, and by 1909 the industry had almost ceased.

In 1869 Shoreham Harbour had 295 fishing boats including 18 of more than 15 tons while 790 were rowing boats. They provided jobs for 740 men and 89 boys. But by 1913 the number of boats had fallen to 184 and the employees to 397. Fish caught included oysters, scallops, whiting, sole and plaice.

Scallop dredging declined in the 1920s through over fishing and a fall in price. Sole, herring and mackerel were still fished after the Second World War but there was only a handful of boats. However scallop fishing has revived since then and Shoreham is the most important port in the country for them.

Fishing has always been a dangerous occupation and there have been a number of tragic incidents involving Shoreham fishermen. Four men were drowned during a sudden squall in 1857 when their barge laden with oysters sank and a man aboard the *Ann Elizabeth* in 1874 was swept overboard during a gale, leaving a wife and five children. A man was swept overboard in 1913 from the deck of the smack *Blue Eyed Minnie* at the harbour entrance. His body was later found on a beach in Brighton.

Shoreham has always been closely connected with Brighton. Many fishermen from the large town preferred to use the canal as a base rather than haul boats up and down the steep shingle beach. But that changed when Brighton built a marina and the fleet is now moored there.

Alan Hayes, a Brighton fisherman, said the advantages of Shoreham seemed obvious compared with having to land boats on the shingle.

Below: Part of the Shoreham oyster beds in 1875. There were others in Southwick. *MM*

More than two dozen fishing boats work from Shoreham catching white fish and shellfish. In the winter, cod and whiting are the favourites with plaice in the spring and sole, turbot, brill and rays in summer. Other catches include crabs, mullet, mussels and gurnard.

In the present century Shoreham emerged as one of England's most significant ports, both for the value of the catch and, especially, for its scallop landings. In 2007, for example, the £6.3m of fish and shellfish landed at Shoreham made it the most important fishery between Brixham in the south west and Scottish east coast ports. The port also became an increasingly important haven and repair centre for vessels registered elsewhere.

Above: Oyster smacks moored in front of the old Malt House and south of Albion Street, 10 October 1889. *JGC*

Left: Beam trawler *Sara Lena* owned by Leach Fishing Enterprises which currently run Brighton and Newhaven Fisheries. *FG*

Power to the people

Shoreham Harbour became the powerhouse for the Brighton area during the late Victorian age with first the gasworks and then an electricity power station being built on the south side. Later a second power station was built so that for a time there were three separate stations near each other.

When gas first started to be used as a fuel, two separate companies were set up to serve Brighton and Hove, one based at Black Rock at the eastern edge of the conurbation and the other next to St Andrew's Old Church in Hove. But it soon became obvious that a bigger site was needed further away from people's homes.

The Brighton and Hove General Gas Company, which operated the Hove site where there was no room to expand, earmarked a seven-acre site south of the canal in 1866 and a Parliamentary Bill was proposed to build it. But there were strong objections from neighbours and a dispute over who owned the land. It took five years, including two court cases, to resolve the issue.

Then the gasworks was built in the 1870s and it was not a thing of beauty. It also produced a powerful odour which was normally taken by the south west wind to affect much of Portslade and Hove. It became known as the Portslade pong. Along the seafront in Hove, property prices increased markedly where the pong could not be detected, from Errol Road and eastward.

THE CANAL, PORTSLADE.

The site soon needed expansion and also required protection from the sea which flooded the plant during a storm in 1875. A second pipeline was constructed to the gasholders in Church Road and the plant was capable of producing 100,000 cubic feet an hour.

Far left: Brighton B power station in 1985. *SPA*

Above: Southwick power station, renamed Brighton A power station in 1948. *SBIT*

Right: Gas workers on the narrow jetty leading to the ferry. The vessel held 40 people and was hauled across the canal to the gasworks by rope. *JGC*

Below right: The ferry at the bottom of Boundary Road. The fare to cross the canal was one penny. The boats carried up to six people and operated until the 1960s. *SBIT*

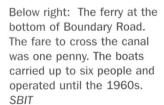

New wharves were needed to satisfy the plant's enormous need for coal that arrived by collier and a second extension was built in the 1890s. The demand for gas was vast even early in the 20th century when electricity was used more widely.

During the First World War most of the men joined the armed forces and the plant was staffed mainly by pensioners and women. No concessions were made to the female workers who got filthy dirty and undertook a lot of lifting. Later in the conflict some prisoners of war were used as labourers. The gasworks also made some bombs and produced benzol for high explosives as part of the war effort.

Most staff at the gasworks lived locally and were ferried across the canal each day in small boats called gassies.

Baltic Wharf and Ferry, Portslade. F142

One has been preserved at the junction of Church Road and Wellington Road in Portslade. The gasworks even had its own fire brigade with 20 men on site.

The work was hard although horses were used to pull the heaviest carts. They were so used to the journey back to their stalls in Portslade that when the evening hooter sounded, they would trot back home of their own accord. The hooter was accurate enough for local people to set their watches and clocks by it.

Coal was unloaded from colliers into carts that were pushed along rails before being shovelled into retorts until a hydraulic wheel was introduced to do this work for them. Sometimes the gas, which was highly toxic, overcame the men and they were given milk to absorb the poison.

Many generations of the same families worked there and the place was a close-knit community. It boasted many sports teams and produced its own concert parties. There was a sports day each year at a recreation ground on the other side of the canal.

At its peak, the plant produced more than 65 million cubic feet of gas a day. It also consumed over four million gallons of water. It was a wasteful process but innovations were made over the years to make it more efficient, including putting waste heat to work in the plant.

Production was scaled down as the end neared for coal gas in the 1960s and natural gas from the North Sea took its place. Production stopped at Portslade in 1971 and 300 men lost their jobs. The gasworks was demolished shortly afterwards.

Top right: The gas workers' annual sports taking place on the recreation ground in the south-east corner of the gasworks site. *SBIT*

Below right: Colliers delivering coal to the gasworks. The *Seaford*, a Stevenson Clark ship, is on the right. *SBIT*

Colliers were specially designed to serve the gasworks at Portslade and had to be small until the new lock at Southwick was built in the 1930s. The capacity was almost doubled from 850 to 1,400 tons of coal. The collier *Pulborough* rescued a yacht in distress off Cuckmere Haven in 1935 which belonged to Alan Herbert, the novelist and MP.

Electricity was produced in Brighton at North Road by the Corporation in its early days but the need for a bigger power station was soon evident. The best site was at the harbour in Southwick, just over the border from the gasworks in Portslade.

Work started in 1902 and a surprise for labourers was finding a derelict ship buried deep on the site. It is believed to have been a vessel that sank when trying to find the old mouth of the harbour. Another tricky task was taking an electric cable from the south to the north side and divers were used to place it under the canal bed.

The building, which cost £350,000, was officially opened in 1906 by John Burns, president of the Local Government Board. He started up the plant amid a ceremony of considerable opulence in the turbine hall which was festooned with flags.

Like the gasworks, the power station was not a good neighbour. Complaints were received constantly from people in Portslade and Southwick about particles of grit from the chimneys. Complainants included two schools and the Star Model Laundry. A contemporary report said the hum it made could be heard in the Old Shoreham Road more than a mile away. It also described the vista from the building looking north as a 'picturesque view across the green-banked canal and the Downs and the woods of Shoreham'.

The fixed transporter unloading coal at the new electric power station, 23 February 1906. *ND*

Below: Brighton B power station with its two chimneys, 360 feet high, towering over the cargo ships at the Inner Lay-By Wharf. *SPA*

Right: Not a job for the faint hearted: a workman removing the soot from the lightning conductors and the rim of power station chimney. *SPA*

The power station was a voracious user of coal and in 1936 the council bought two colliers. The *Arthur Wright* was named after the first manager and engineer of the works, and the other was called *Henry Moon*, after the alderman who chaired the lighting committee. Although the *Henry Moon* was sunk during the Second World War, the *Arthur Wright* stayed in service until 1963 when she was sold to a firm in Norway.

There was a big ceremony in 1936 when the *Arthur Wright* made her maiden voyage. Coal handlers, for once looking clean at work, were ready to help dignitaries as they gingerly made their way on to the gang plank after she had sailed down the canal decorated with flags. One woman slipped, dropping her leather handbag into the water and without a moment's hesitation, crane driver Harry Short jumped into the freezing water to retrieve it. He returned the bag through a colleague, who dried it, to the lady who offered a reward of half a crown.

Eventually the power station became known as Brighton A when after the war a second one was commissioned to cope with demand. Electricity had now been nationalised and was no longer run by the Corporation, much to the regret of many staff.

The new power station, Brighton B, was a massive building, looking like Battersea in south London. Started in 1947, it needed 5,000 piles for the foundations and contained 15 million bricks. The twin chimneys at 360 feet high made it the tallest building in Sussex. They could be seen from the Isle of Wight on a clear day. Together, the two power stations covered an area of 45 acres.

Brighton B could produce 330 megawatts once fully open in 1952. It needed a fleet of colliers on permanent duty to bring in the coal and they became a familiar sight in the harbour. They were some of the last steam driven ships in service off the British coast. They were called *Sir John Snell*, *Charles H Merz*, *Sir William Walker* and *James Rowan* after prominent men in the electricity supply industry. Each collier could carry 3,400 tons and at least one could always be seen at the harbour.

Brighton B discharged warm water into the English Channel and the dock, a process that required close co-operation with the Harbour Board. One problem was the danger for bathers nearby wishing to take advantage of the heat. During the 1970s, two girls died tragically after ignoring warning notices.

The ancient Brighton A was run down in the 1960s and closed completely in 1976. There was a closing ceremony, not nearly as joyous as the opening had been 70 years earlier. Its twin chimneys at 250 feet high were demolished using dynamite and the rest of the building followed in 1980. A souvenir brochure said: 'One could only marvel that the station, with much of the original building, had remained a viable proposition for more than 70 years.'

Brighton B was also becoming antiquated and closed in 1988 with the loss of 330 jobs. The conurbation then received power from elsewhere via the National Grid.

Thousands of people watched the eastern chimney being blown up in 1988 and the turbine hall was demolished two years later. The second chimney was demolished in 1998, again to big crowds after a vain attempt to save it as a local landmark.

In the late 1990s gas made a reappearance when a new electric power station was built at the harbour. This needed a gas pipeline from the station near Devil's Dyke to Southwick. The operators, Scottish Power, South Coast Power and Seeboard, paid £1.25 million to the community as compensation for disruption. Among the projects to benefit were the South Portslade community centre, St Helens's Church at Hangleton and the paddling pool at Hove Lagoon

Work started on this £200 million replacement in 1999 and it started producing electricity in 2000. One of the most efficient in Britain, its single chimney is only 20 feet lower than the two at Brighton B. Its single generator has a greater output than the six in the old building.

Not many people going along the busy A259 in Southwick know there is a tunnel under the canal. It was built to run a water main and other services to Brighton B and is now used to take the gas main to the new power station.

The current power station has, like its predecessors, become another local landmark, with its 230 foot chimney lit at night. *SPA*

A powerful end

Work started on the Brighton B power station in 1947. The first generating set was commissioned in 1952 and the last in 1958 when the station was completed. It was constructed next to the 1906 Brighton A station to help keep up with the demand for electricity. These pictures were taken in 1988 when the first chimney was blown up as crowds watched along the banks of the canal. The generating hall was then demolished but the west chimney remained as a landmark for another ten years. Early on a Sunday morning in the autumn of 1998 that chimney too was blown up. *SPA*

Far right: The third power station which started producing electricity in 2000. *SPA*

COBBY
SHOREHAM

A KNOTTY QUESTION.

The pilots

by Ken Wilcox

Ships visiting unfamiliar coasts and ports need skilled local mariners to assist and guide them. Pilots have provided this service to mariners for centuries.

Little detail is known about the pilots up to 1760, when the modern port began to be established. However they were active, and an unregulated service certainly existed. Warships built at the end of the 17th century used their services to navigate the difficult river passage of some three miles from New Shoreham to the sea.

After 1808, under Trinity House, the new regulator, pilots were self employed, maintained their own boats and regulated their own internal affairs. They were supervised by the local pilotage sub-committee that reported any serious incidents, agreed tariffs charged to ships and enforced policy.

Pilots had a fit for service annual review and were charged a guinea to renew their licence before the sub-committee. At one time Trinity House tried to simplify the fee and charge £1 but the pilots objected, preferring to pay the traditional guinea. For a pilot to pay more than was necessary was indeed unusual!

The everyday life of a pilot then as now can be difficult and dangerous. Boarding or landing from the pilot boat to and from ships in bad weather is often hazardous. The work would not be possible without the coxswains and crews. Hours of work for all concerned are unsocial and relate to the ever-changing tide that rules the passage of all ships. During the 19th century each pilot had his own boat and the first pilot to a ship in the offing secured the job. This led to some dubious practices but eventually a roster was adopted to share the work and pilot boats more fairly.

Far left: Five pilots in front of old lifeboat house. From left: M Hatcher, W Cobby, W Young, F Grant and S Upperton, circa 1900. *MM*

Left: The *Travemar Africa*, a cargo vessel manoeuvring in the eastern arm of the harbour assisted by the tug *Adurni* with pilot cutter No 4 standing by. *SPA*

Squeezed between the two lifeboat houses just west of Kingston beach, the now demolished pilots' watch house, shown in a mid-20th century photograph, was an unusual looking building with crenellations. *MM*

In 1855, when the new lock at Southwick was opened, the eight serving pilots bought the first steam paddle tug to be registered at the port. Named *Don*, she served for four years before being replaced by the *Pilots*, a new paddle tug built for the pilots in 1859 at South Shields. Both tugs were involved in salvage claims for assisting ships off Shoreham. The pilots seem to have held the towage rights until the 1870s when the reformed Port Authority acquired a new tug from R H Penney, the new chairman and local ship-owner. She was named *Stella* and served the port for some 50 years.

Pilots were very experienced mariners, typically fishermen or officers and sometimes masters from the merchant service. Many had outside interests in the 19th century although they were barred by law from being a licensee! The tug is one example where earnings were diversified by associated activities. The Brazier family had interests in the oyster fishery while the Merrix family had shares in collier brigs. Owning shares in ships was a common investment in 19th century maritime communities.

Late in the 19th century, pilots served in the local lifeboat provided by the newly formed RNLI. Robert Brazier, a master mariner and licensed pilot, lost his life in 1874, being drowned when the lifeboat capsized whilst on exercise in the harbour entrance. The same entrance had claimed the lives of three pilots in 1837: William Dyer, John Hide and George Bungard were all drowned when the pilot boat capsized returning from boarding a Norwegian schooner off the port. Francis Child, a pilot and Master Mariner, was tragically killed by a parting towrope later in the century. Again in 1968 the service suffered another sad loss when Len Pilcher fell from the pilot ladder and was drowned whilst trying to board a ship off the port. These heartbreaking losses were not only felt by the families but were shared by the whole port community. Modern pilot boats and improved safety equipment have reduced many of the risks associated with pilotage but unfortunately they can never be totally eradicated.

By 1898 the pilots had a watch house on Kingston Beach close to the lifeboat house and in later years used a top room in the lifeboat house for this purpose. Their own boats were kept close by, hauled up on the beach.

The new century heralded change both for the pilots and for the port. Two new locks and two new power stations in the space of 50 years increased trade, particularly of coal.

After the building of Brighton B power station and the Prince Philip lock, together with the associated improvements in the entrance during the 1950s, the pilots moved to a watch house situated south of the locks. New pilots were required to have a Foreign Going Master Mariners Certificate in view of the larger ships using the port. In 1988 a new Pilotage Act came into force transferring responsibility for the provision of pilotage services from Trinity House to the Shoreham Port Authority.

There are now five employed pilots, reflecting the reduction in shipping movements following the loss of the two power stations in 1976 and 1987 and the decreasing river traffic brought about by residential development. Their professionalism and dedication reflect that of their previous Trinity House colleagues. All are proud to have delivered a first class pilotage service to the ships using Shoreham and to have contributed to the efficient operation of the port.

Above left: Pilot boats 3 and 4 on 9 August 1984. *KenW*

Above: Shoreham pilots in 1984: from the left they are W Ryder, I Forsaith, R Ball, J Rudd, K Wilcox, E Wray (senior pilot), L Cate, T R Mowatt and M Liley. *KenW*

Left: The view from a pilot boat having boarded a pilot on the cargo ship *Independent*. *SPA*

The harbour surroundings

Shoreham Harbour is obviously a major feature in the town which shares its name but arguably has had an even bigger effect on its neighbours, Southwick and Portslade, which also have a frontage to the port.

Southwick, which actually contains the harbour mouth, has access to its beach only over the locks while Portslade has no direct access within the town at all to its beach now that ferries no longer cross the canal. Apart from works boats transporting gasworks employees across the canal, other ferry services in the past included the *Jolly Boatman* and two local firms, A Ford and Hamlin. Rowing boats could also be hired from local boatyards for pleasure trips on the canal waters.

Both Southwick and Portslade started as villages away from the coast before extending southwards in the 19th century to become industrial towns. They each developed shopping streets parallel to the canal. In Southwick, Albion Street is actually part of the A259 while in Portslade North Street is one block back. North Street slowly lost its shops to nearby Boundary Road and Station Road as the direct impact of the port lessened, while Albion Street was earmarked for widening in the 1960s. One side was pulled down for a scheme that never took place which is why there is a large green area in front of the coast road flats. Also at this time, the shops moved to a purpose-built centre in Southwick Square.

Doris Randall, who grew up early last century, lived in Adur Terrace, part of the main coast road. She remembered as a five year old being able to cross the road by herself because there was so little traffic, reaching the grassy bank and jumping on to firm sand by the canal.

Far left: The first Norfolk Bridge constructed in 1833. *MM*

Above: 'Shoreham Harbour' by H G Hine, 1850. *MM*

Right: Luxury yachts moored in front of Albion Street, Southwick, now the site of the Lady Bee Marina. *SPA*

Far right: Buildings that survived 1960s redevelopment included the 19th-century Malt House and Schooner Inn and the 1906 Town Hall. *SPA*

Below: Shoreham Beach and Harbour in 1965. *SPA*

There was then a narrow strip of beach between the canal and the sea. The harbour entrance had old wooden piers and the Victorian fort on the other side of the river was a favourite place for picnics.

In its prime, North Street was a busy road, catering for hundreds of workers at the gasworks and electricity power stations on the other side of the canal. It even boasted a couple of cinemas. Little trace remains of all this activity as during the 1960s this street was also widened to cater mainly for light industrial buildings.

There was a full set of local shops selling sweets, meat, vegetables, clothes, ice and second hand goods. North Street also housed a popular café, several pubs and a Salvation Amy citadel.

Originally the coastal road ran below the low cliffs but was affected greatly by erosion. Then in 1781 a turnpike road was built along the cliff top leading to an increase in traffic. The building of the railway in 1840 separated both South Portslade and Southwick from their old village centres.

In the mid-19th century there was a twice-daily horse bus service from Shoreham to Brighton. This was augmented in the 1880s by the launch of a horse tram service which started at the Swiss Gardens pleasure grounds in Shoreham and went to Westbourne Villas where Hove's boundary began in those days. An electric tram service started in Brighton in 1901 but Hove never allowed trams to cross its territory. The Brighton to Shoreham tramway stopped in 1913 and was the first in the country to have succumbed to competition from buses.

Many pubs were established in the area to cater mainly for thirsty workers in the port and sailors on shore leave. While in Portslade they tended to take all sorts of names, in Southwick they reflected history. They included the Victory (built after the Battle of Trafalgar in 1805) and the Railway Tavern. The Sir Robert Napier was named after a military hero while the Shipwrights' Arms, the Sawyers' Arms, the Mariners' Arms, the Pilot, the Schooner and the Sea House all had nautical connotations reflecting the locality.

The Crown at Copperas Gap catered for workers in the harbour between the 1830s and its demolition in 1969. Another pub on the coast road which kept going until recently was the Half Way House in Wellington Road, the mid point between Shoreham and Brighton. Two pubs opposite each other on the A259 at Fishersgate used to have rowing races on the canal, the King's Head and the Sussex.

Albion Street had all the local provisions shops plus some which catered for sailors such as the ships' chandlery established by A O Muggeridge. There was also a depot for the

horse-drawn trams. A new town hall was built in 1906 after Southwick had become an urban district and the red-bricked edifice is still there today although no longer in civic use.

Southwick's most celebrated daughter was Clara Butt who became a much-admired singer. A plaque was later put on her birthplace in Adur Terrace. Her father was an oyster dredgerman and she was baptised in 1872 at the Methodist chapel on top of a sail loft. Clara's family left Southwick when she was two. She later became world famous for her powerful voice. She was made a Dame during the First World War for her work in entertaining the troops and died in 1936.

The Adur above the footbridge looking east with a yacht alongside the Town Quay. In 1928, Michael Paget Baxter of 1 Seaside Villas and owner of harbour land, commissioned the artist John Powell to complete nine paintings of the port. These paintings belonged to M P Baxter's son Peter Marsh. *PM*

Below: Southwick regatta, 1914. *SBIT*

Above right: The lagoon before it was landscaped in the 1930s. The scratched-out writing advertised the Seaside Villas to let furnished. *SBIT*

Below right: A seaplane in Aldrington Basin in front of the Seaside Villas. The houses were built for Michael Paget Baxter who lived in one and rented out the others. *SBIT*

Hove contains the way in to the south side of the canal through Wharf Road and Basin Road South. There have been many plans to replace this awkward and unprepossessing entrance by taking part of the nearby park or by creating a new entrance opposite the foot of Church Road but nothing has yet happened. Hove Lagoon was built on old mud flats, at times the mouth of the river. The coast road is mainly residential on the north side with a few bed and breakfast houses catering for lorry drivers using the harbour. Basin Road North contains many small businesses.

Shoreham Harbour's influence on Brighton has been as its nearest port – three miles away from the eastern end as compared with almost five to Newhaven from the borough

THE BASIN PORTSLADE.

boundary. When the Marina was built in the 1970s, it took some small boats but not many. The yacht basins at Shoreham continued to thrive.

The harbour has always been the main source of employment, greatly exceeding the second biggest at Shoreham Airport. It also has a far longer harbour frontage than Hove, Portslade or Southwick. Because Shoreham faces the river

SOUTHWICK REGATTA - 1914 -

BENSLY & CO COAL SHIPPERS. 14 WESTERN RD HOVE.

rather than the canal, it sees little commercial shipping but there is a thriving colony of about 40 houseboats on the south side. Some of them were built locally during the Second World War. There is also much new private housing by the river.

Shoreham has five bridges over the Adur. The most southerly is the Dolphin footbridge built in the 1920s to connect Shoreham to the beach and Bungalow Town from Dolphin Hard. It was opened in 1921 by Earl Winterton, MP. Narrow and ugly, it is soon to be replaced and improved.

The oldest is the toll bridge, now pedestrianised, which used to carry the A27 over the Adur. First opened in 1782, it was rebuilt in the 20th century. Although 500 feet long, it is only 12 feet wide and when traffic used it, the bridge was controlled by

lights. It closed in 1970 when the Shoreham flyover was built. The bridge has been renovated after falling into a poor state.

Carrying the A259 across the river, the Norfolk Bridge has been rebuilt several times. It first opened in 1833 as a suspension bridge and was opened by the Duke of Norfolk. A replacement in 1923, which was much uglier, was itself superseded by the current bridge in 1987.The railway bridge has been there since the line was extended from Shoreham to Worthing in the 1840s although the current structure is not the original. Finally the A27 crosses the river on a box girder bridge.

Above: Stained glass window in St Julian's Church at Kingston, 'In memory of Albert Holloway drowned at sea Oct 1919 aged 67'. *FG*

Left: Workmen constructing the second Norfolk Bridge in 1923. *MM*

Safeguarding the port

Britain enjoyed a prolonged period of peace in the century from the end of the Napoleonic wars to the outbreak of the First World War. But as a major nation in the world, she had to keep vigilant.

In the 1840s, the harbour commissioners asked the Prime Minister Lord John Russell how they should protect the port in case of war. The thinking was that any invader would seek to storm the south coast.

Nothing happened then but the more warlike Lord Palmerston was greatly concerned about the possibility in the following decade. The Government took over spare land on the west side of the west pier to build a fort.

This was duly built and equipped much to everyone's satisfaction but like many other forts constructed at this time, it never saw any action. The main battle was between the commissioners and the War Office over a wooden hut on the west pier that the Army felt would be in the way of any gunfire. It had to go and it did.

The fort cost more than £11,000, a large sum then, and it was well equipped. Overlooking the harbour, it would have been effective had the French decided to invade. During the Second World War, it was again equipped for action but once more there was no invasion.

Today the fort on Shoreham Beach is open to the public. It was restored in 1978 and 2004. There are notice boards explaining its history and entrance is free. It is a scheduled ancient monument

Lights were placed on the piers from the earliest days to enable ships to enter the harbour safely and a lighthouse was built on the middle pier in 1820. In 1846 a permanent replacement was built on the shore at Kingston and it is still there today.

Far left: Shoreham lifeboat *Hermione Lady Colwyn* with crew and coastguard rescue helicopter, 4 October 2009. *RNLI*

Below: 1956 view showing the older fort designed to protect the harbour entrance. *SPA*

Top right: The lighthouse was built in 1846. The lighting technology has moved on and two of the earlier lights are preserved in the Marlipins Museum and Southwick Manor Cottage. *ND*

KINGSTON LIGHTHOUSE, SOUTHWICK.

In its early days, the lighthouse used the best sperm oil for the beam. It came from whales and was considered to give the greatest glow. But in 1875 it was converted to gas which was cheaper and easier to use. Today it is powered by electricity which was installed in 1952. The lighthouse was restored in 1986 and in 2009. It now uses lower cost power and gives out a brighter light.

Shoreham lifeboat used to be run by the commissioners but in 1865 the Royal National Lifeboat Institution took over the service including the boat called the *Ramonet*, which stayed in service until 1890. Apart from a five year gap between 1924 and 1929, the lifeboat has operated ever since. The Shoreham lifeboat took part in the Second World War, helping to rescue men from Dunkirk.

In 2007 the RNLI launched an appeal for £1 million towards the cost of a new lifeboat station. Almost half that sum was raised in the first two years. It was needed because the old lifeboat station, demolished in 2009, was built in 1933 for a boat weighing eight tonnes. The present boat weighs 28 tonnes and caused the old slipway to crack.

The lifeboat is one of the busiest on the south coast and it is intended that the new station should be able to operate for at least the next 50 years.

Shoreham hosted the Maritime Volunteer Service covering an area from the eastern arm of Brighton Marina to Sea Lane, Ferring. They were housed in a tower built on the fort in the 1960s. It has since become derelict and they now operate from a different site. National Coastwatch, also volunteer based, had a former searchlight station restored for it by the port.

Right: The new lifeboat house under construction in May 2010. It will have a larger boat hall, crew training room, viewing platform, changing and drying facilities. *FG*

Lifeboats

Top left: The old lifeboat house, early 20th century. *MM*

Above: Crew of the lifeboat standing to attention while *Balmoral* passes at the opening of Prince Phillip Lock, 1958. *SPA*

Bottom left: Prince George at the opening ceremony of the new lifeboat house and boat in 1933. *SPA*

Bottom right: Shoreham lifeboat crew, 2004. *RNLI*

Diverse divers

Above: Diver Horace Weller working on Prince George Lock in 1932. *SPA*

Above right: Diver Keith Wadey about to fix a power duct, winter 1980. *KW*

Bottom right: This diving equipment, Siebe Gorman 12 bolt standard dress, was used at the port for the last time in June 1983. *KW*

Bottom left: Valkyrie Diving Services team in preparation 2009. *KW*

A recent view of the harbour entrance. The East Breakwater Spur was added in 1990 after the Outer Lay-By Terminal was enlarged.
SPA

WHILE SOUTHWICK SLEEPS THE NAVAL MONSTERS GROW

Wartime

People in Shoreham were surprised to see two huge towers being built in the harbour from June 1918 during the First World War. They became known as the Mystery Towers because of the great secrecy surrounding them.

More than 3,000 civilians and 5,000 soldiers worked on the project and the eventual cost of the towers was more than £1 million each. They were 180 feet high and contained 9,000 tons of concrete.

They were intended to form part of a line of 12 towers that would have been sunk on to a shoal in the Dover Straits between Dungeness and Cap Gris Nez. The towers would have been linked by steel boom nets to block the path for German U boats. On the top were guns and men would also have been stationed there.

Shoreham was chosen because it had a suitable area of calm water and good links by rail. But the Armistice was signed only five months later with the two towers not quite finished. Work had started on another three.

They remained in place for another two years until one of them was floated out of Shoreham almost 40 miles west to form what is now the Nab Tower near the Isle of Wight. The second tower was demolished which was just as well since it was six feet too wide to have passed through the harbour mouth. The concrete was broken up and used as foundations for housing and greenhouses.

There was no enemy action in Shoreham Harbour during the First World War but the conflict did have a severe effect on trade. Revenue dropped from £10,366 in 1913 to £4,564 in 1917. In 1918 Brighton Council lent the trustees £5,000 and in 1920 the port raised dues by 100 per cent to attempt to ease its financial problems.

Far left: Mystery Towers. *SBIT*

Below: Men from the 92nd Field Company on their catamaran bridge across the canal by the gasworks. *SBIT*

The mystery towers revealed

'While Southwick sleeps the naval monsters grow'. Photographer Joseph Gurney Ridley produced over 90 different postcards of the Mystery Towers while they were at Southwick. Some carried slogans: 'Excuse me what are they building here', 'The new naval wonder' and 'Reinforced concrete foundations'.

Above left: A large crowd watches one of the Mystery Towers being towed out of the harbour, 12 September 1920. *SBIT*

Above: A curious view of the lighthouse with the Mystery Towers behind, taken from Kingston beach. *SBIT*

Left: An aerial view illustrating how the huge towers dominated the harbour. *SBIT*

The gasworks were used to produce bombs, and benzol, used for making high explosives. Nearly all the employees of military age joined up, so the company had to employ 150 women, boys and pensioners. Later, German prisoners of war were employed despite local objections. Assurances were given that the prisoners would not be allowed in the gas making plant and they were taken to work daily under armed guard to remove clinkers. The end of the war in 1918 was signalled by sounding the hooter at the gasworks.

During the Second World War, the harbour was taken over by the armed forces because of Shoreham's important strategic position. Albion Street on the north side was restricted with road blocks of beach huts at each end. People needed passes to enter the area. Old vessels were kept in the port to be sunk near the harbour mouth in case of invasion. An ancient wooden boat called the *Seven Sisters* was used to block the canal. Small boys used to swim out to her from the canal bank on hot days.

The beaches were mined and covered with barbed wire. As a defence measure, many houses on Shoreham Beach were demolished and their residents evacuated. Some ships were stationed at the Lady Bee Marina where torpedo boats and at least one submarine were also repaired.

Shoreham Harbour was also used as a training ground for cadet ratings at HMS King Alfred in Hove. This had been built before the war as swimming baths. When it returned to civilian use, it retained the wartime name and still operates today as a leisure centre. The Germans were confused about the King Alfred and at one time claimed to have sunk her.

Some of the ratings were based at Lancing College. More than 22,500 passed through the King Alfred during the war, among them Ludovic Kennedy, Sir Michael Hordern, Sir Alec Guinness, Sir Peter Scott, Richard Baker, Kenneth More and Ross and Norris McWhirter.

NAVAL MOTOR LAUNCHES IN SOUTHWICK HARBOUR

Several small ships including the lifeboat were used in the Dunkirk rescue bid in 1940. A race held by the Southwick and Shoreham Yacht Club was cancelled so that skippers could take their ships to France. Members of the Sussex Yacht Club went a few days later to St Valery in a bid to rescue trapped servicemen there.

Shoreham was also one of the ports used by smaller vessels for the Normandy landings in 1944. Some people recall seeing them in the harbour waiting for D-Day. The port was used for the earlier, ill-fated Dieppe raid in 1942 in which thousands of troops, many Canadian, were killed or captured.

Much secrecy surrounded the harbour in wartime but Southwick people did welcome the arrival of Canadian naval officers. They were much better supplied with rations than their British counterparts and often gave chocolate bars to children.

Naval motor launches moored alongside the quay at Southwick with the fishing boats and large yachts, post-1918. *SBIT*

DREDGING IN SHOREHAM HARBOUR IN VIEW OF MINE NO.0/0116/13 OF 4TH FEBRUARY 1943.

(Resident Naval Officer, Shoreham's No.066/1454 dated 6th May, 1943)

- -

III

No.0/0115/93/a
NAVAL OFFICER-IN-CHARGE, NEWHAVEN.
(Copies to:-
    Captain, H.M.S. VERNON.
    Resident Naval Officer, Shoreham).

    Approval is given to lift the cables and the observation mines in the entrance to Shoreham Harbour as proposed in Minute I.

    2.   Opportunity should be taken for any necessary refitting of gear and overhaul of mines to be taken in hand during dredging operations.

    3.   It is requested that you will make arrangements direct with H.M.S. VERNON for the required work to be carried out informing the Commander-in-Chief of the proposed programme and estimated date of completion.

    4.   The mines should not be replaced pending a decision on the question of whether an observation minefield is to be retained at Shoreham.

(Sd.) CHARLES LITTLE

Portsmouth.
26th May 1943.

Admiral.

IV

No.2656/0/0115/93
ADMIRALTY.

    Forwarded for the information of Their Lordships with reference to Admiralty Letter M.052828/43 of 20th May 1943, para.3 (c).

Shoreham did not escape bomb damage and five bombs were dropped on the harbour during a raid in August 1940. One of the planes was hit by shots from a gun at the port and it crashed into the sea. No one was killed and there was little damage. The German planes were returning from a bombing raid north of Shoreham and had some bombs to jettison before flying home. A second set of bombs in September demolished a coal shed, sending scores of wooden planks into the air. A third bombing raid in November killed 17-year-old butcher's boy, William Wood, as he delivered meat to a ship. Also that year, aircraft attacked and sank the *Henry Moon* electricity works collier and the *Portslade*, which served the gasworks. In another raid the *Shell Brit* was bombed while berthed at Shell Wharf.

Four bombs were dropped on the gasworks in September 1940, wrecking the coal stores but not affecting production. The only casualty was a horse. Some drivers had to dive under their lorries as the bombs fell, Two months later the gasworks was targeted in another raid and one man was hit in the head by shrapnel but survived.

The power station was an obvious target for bombs despite an effort to camouflage it but there were surprisingly few attacks and it kept working throughout the war. The most serious raid was in 1942 when one man was killed and ten were injured. There were another three raids that year.

Shoreham Harbour was used as a combined operations landing craft base when *HMS Lizard* was opened in July 1942 to act as a training and re-supply depot.

One of a series of letters between the resident Naval Officer at Shoreham and the Naval Officer in charge at Newhaven in 1943, seeking approval for removing the observation minefield between the piers at Shoreham harbour to allow dredging. *TNA*

It was at Butt's Baltic Wharf on Aldrington Basin, providing training for men of the Royal Marines and Royal Navy in seamanship and survival skills to prepare them for their hazardous duties as landing craft crews.

HMS Lizard occupied buildings at several sites in the Shoreham and Hove area. Many of them were at the bottom of Grand Avenue including the Princes Hotel (now the headquarters of Brighton and Hove City Council), and Courtenay Gate.

Crews took part in regular exercises, usually up the coast to the sister landing craft base, *HMS Newt* in Newhaven. However crews, were not always given advance warnings, particularly of night exercises. Often men were awoken in the middle of the night and loaded on to Southdown buses waiting outside to transport them to their craft moored in the Portslade canal.

HMS Lizard handled hundreds of landing craft during its three years in service. It played a major role in both the Dieppe raid and the D-Day operation. The base began to run down towards eventual closure after VJ Day on August 15 1945 and closed at the end of the year. During its period of operation it had trained 50,000 men.

Plan of World War II bomb damage to the West Pier of harbour. *FG*

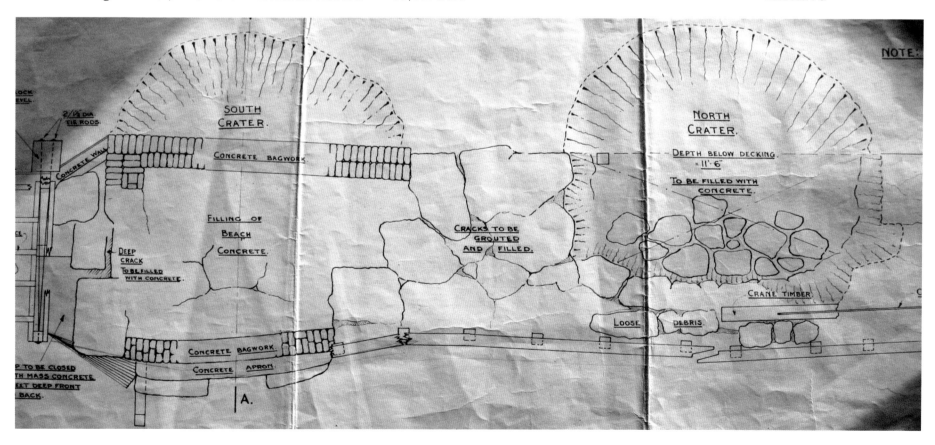

Dreams and schemes

Politicians and developers have fixed their beady eyes on Shoreham Harbour ever since the Second World War, believing it represents a huge opportunity in a land locked area. The harbour is often said to be the biggest brownfield site in the south east but that includes land not within the boundaries of the port.

But there have been two difficulties that have prevented any major schemes from reaching fruition. One is road access. To reach the main trunk road network at Benfield Valley, the choice is either an expensive tunnel or widening existing roads involving the demolition of many homes.

The other problem is that the port has straddled two counties and several districts. At one time, any major scheme in the port had to be considered by both East and West Sussex County Councils and three urban district councils in Portslade, Southwick and Shoreham plus a borough council in Hove. And then for good measure, Brighton, only three miles away, also had to be included.

Streamlining of local government has lessened the bureaucracy but port development still has to be considered by Brighton and Hove City Council, the county council at West Sussex, and Adur District Council.

In the 1980s, there were plans for a passenger ferry terminal that would have rivalled that at Newhaven. This led to strong objections from neighbours and from councils worried about the likely congestion, traffic and noise. There were also problems because Shoreham is tidal. Eventually the project was dropped in 1987. In 1994 the idea was revived with the audacious proposal of moving ferries to Dieppe from Newhaven but again it came to nothing.

Councils collaborated in the early 1990s on a major study for improving road access to the port but could not reach agreement. Hove objected vociferously to a link to the A27 through Vale Park, Portslade cemetery and the Victoria Recreation Ground, which would have involved some property demolition. It also did not like the idea of widening Church Road and Trafalgar Road, leading to demolishing even more homes and blighting those remaining. Adur opposed a link at Fishersgate, passing through allotments and playing fields. All three schemes were dropped.

Road access problems were revived in 1998 when international planner Graham Moss was hired to produce a master plan for the port. He envisaged a maritime village at the western end, port activities concentrated around the harbour entrance and a media village at the Hove and Portslade end. The idea of the road tunnel was mooted at this point but abandoned because of the cost. Although the scheme had some attractive features, it foundered for familiar reasons.

Far left: Photograph taken at 12pm on 5 March 1954. The chemical works can be seen on the south bank of the western arm. *SPA*

Above: Luxury yachts moored along the harbour at Southwick, circa 1914. The Lady Bee Marina occupies the area today. *ND*

Right: Sussex Yacht Club at Shoreham was founded in 1892 at Southwick. The 1816 Malt House at Southwick is also part of the club. *SPA*

There were plans for a wind farm at the harbour in 1993 with 15 turbines but these were rejected by both Hove and Adur councils. Later that year a second application was made for a smaller scheme of four turbines. There were still objections on account of noise and height. The turbines would have been nearly 200 feet high. A public inquiry was held into the project in 1994 and the plans were rejected by the inspector the following year.

The new combined council in Brighton and Hove had radical ideas for Shoreham in the late 1990s. One scheme, proposed by the leader, Lord Bassam, was for a rapid transit link or monorail along the seafront from Shoreham Harbour to Brighton Marina. This would have opened up access to the port and provided a fast, public transport coastal link. Another advantage was serving proposed new developments such as a regenerated Brighton Centre, a new West Pier, a rebuilt King Alfred leisure

centre in Hove, ice rinks at Black Rock and further development in the Marina. But the scheme did not meet the criteria laid down by the proposed funder, the Millennium Lottery, and it was abandoned.

The council, along with East Sussex County Council, also identified the harbour as a possible site for a waste incinerator in 1998. Among the objectors was broadcaster and newspaper editor Derek Jameson who lived in Hove Seaside Villas close to the port. With others, he formed the Association of Harbour Communities to oppose the scheme and keep an eye on any other activities. But Lord Bassam, unwilling to involve the authority in prolonged controversy, withdrew the idea in 1999.

After moving to the villas in Western Esplanade in Hove, known locally as Millionaires' Row, Jameson became concerned

there was no body representing local people in their views on port developments. Through the Association, he made representations on many schemes including plans for an asphalt plant near the housing.

The Association was successful in ensuring that lorries carrying grit were covered. It also vigorously opposed any major changes proposed for Southwick Beach and is still active today.

Jameson sold his home to Heather Mills and Sir Paul McCartney after retiring from broadcasting in 2001. Other celebrities including Mills, Nick Berry, June Penn, Fatboy Slim and Zoe Ball continue to live in the villas.

Shoreham Harbour was also one of eight sites under consideration by Southern Water for a new sewage treatment works. This also raised strong local objections, as Adur District Council and its residents did not see why they had to deal with the city's waste in addition to their own. There is already a local outfall and treatment works in the harbour. But the main factor against it was the enormous cost of linking it to the main city sewer and Southern Water opted for a site in Peacehaven instead.

Over the years there have been many other proposals for the port. These ideas have included a plant making pellets out of rubbish to produce fuel, a desalination plant producing both fresh water and salt from the sea, a stadium for Brighton and Hove Albion, a combined heat and power scheme providing free electricity for the neighbourhood and a huge housing development at the Aldrington Basin end of the harbour.

A concerted effort to deal with Shoreham Harbour regeneration was made by all the councils together with the port authority and Seeda, the South East England Development Agency. It included ambitious proposals for up to 10,000 homes within the harbour confines or nearby. But Seeda ran out of money in 2009 for the preparatory work and the project was put on hold. In the meantime, councils tried to take the project further and there were suggestions it could become one of the Government's proposed eco towns.

The residential Emerald Quay and South Wharf apartments stand on the site of the chemical works over looking the harbour. *SPA*

Shoreham port today

Visit the port now and it is a bustling place with a wide variety. It has diversified so that it is not reliant on one single trade and it makes full use of its position close to continental Europe.

Shoreham does not compete with major ports such as Southampton capable of handling huge vessels. But it handles cargo efficiently and has thriving fishing and leisure interests. It also has a busy property portfolio.

It is a major port for timber, aggregates, steel, oil, cereals and scrap metal. Shoreham imports about 440,000 cubic metres of timber each year, mainly from Scandinavia and the Baltic states. It has large areas of covered storage and a highly efficient stock control system.

Shoreham has three terminals for aggregates operated by Dudman, Solent Aggregates and the CemexRMC group, importing a million tonnes annually, mainly for road building and making concrete. Most of the material arriving in the port comes from the Isle of Wight area which provides good quality sand and gravel.

The port began importing structural steel in 2007 and handles 20,000 tonnes a year at a specially built terminal. It also imports steel rods and specialist cargoes. Shoreham is home to European Metal Recycling, a huge concern operating its own terminal to export scrap steel. Other firms export metal, mainly to Spain and Portugal.

Far left: Looking east down the canal from the locks with the Lady Bee Marina on the left. *FG*

Left: Greenheart hardwood timber fenders being fitted on to the north wall of Prince George Lock, July 2009. *SPA*

Above: Cargo ships discharging at the eastern end of the canal. *SPA*

Right: The red brick building next to the lock is a pump house used for supplying water to the power station and replenishing water to the canal, replacing that lost while operating the lock. *SPA*

Another notable export is grain which goes to countries including Spain and Holland. Some is sent to Scotland where it is used to make malt whisky. It is stored in silos before being shipped out of the port.

Shoreham also imports more than 200,000 tonnes of petroleum products at the Texaco terminal which has been there for many years. It is a fast, efficient and safe operation.

The port authority is now based in Nautilus House, a renovated building in the heart of the harbour overlooking both the locks and Albion Street.

It is in control of an area stretching from the old toll bridge in Shoreham to half way along Hove Lagoon and extending roughly half a mile out to sea. It owns a sizeable commercial portfolio and has 70 tenants ranging from small offices to major firms. There are dozens of small businesses in Quayside House, the

Hove Enterprise Centre and the Lady Bee Marina. Large firms include Tarmac, Texaco, Parker Steel, South Coast Power, Skip IT, Asphaltic, Shoreham Silo Services and B & N Fish Sales.

Proof of the authority's continuing commitment to improvement is the investment in three new covered terminals which have a capacity equal to that of the Albert Hall in London. The port has also improved paving in part of the harbour by putting down five million blocks.

It is the busiest port in the south east for fish with landings totalling 2,500 tonnes worth £6 million made annually. Shoreham has a good reputation for scallops and vessels come from other parts of Britain to fish for them. Berths for fishing boats have been improved.

Yachting plays an important part in leisure at the harbour. There are over 550 small boats moored there, mostly in the Lady Bee Marina, and they make more than 5,000 journeys each year through the locks. However a major plan to renovate the north bank of the canal at Southwick which would have enhanced leisure amenities was rejected by Adur District Council.

A feature of Shoreham port over the years has been good industrial relations and there is also a strong sense of loyalty

Fighting the sea

Top left: Rebuilding the rock groyne after the winter storms of 2004. *KW*

Above: Sections of rock shipped over from France being lowered into position from a barge to make a rock groyne in 2001. *KW*

Left: Also part of the rock groyne work in 2001, shingle being pumped from below the low water mark up on to the beach. *KW*

among employees. Many of the port's workers, including stevedores, pilots, divers and managers, have devoted their working lives to the harbour.

Shoreham is a Trust port run by a Board that replaced the old harbour trustees in 1968. It makes a surplus, which is reinvested, and has survived the recession well. The port is keenly aware of its place in the local community, sponsoring local football teams, holding open days and making sure it maintains clean safe beaches.

The port also replaces beach groynes and steps, maintains harbour patrols, and twice yearly moves 40,000 tonnes of shingle from the western arm to the eastern arm beach, to assist in the littoral drift.

The port works closely with all its stakeholders, particularly the three local authorities of Adur, Brighton and Hove and West Sussex. Regeneration of the Harbour continues to be a goal and the Port Authority is preparing a Port Master Plan to guide the port's activities over the next two to three decades. Shoreham remains a leading niche port in the south east of England, providing exceptional service to its customers, through friendly staff and outstanding infrastructure and facilities.

The two aerial photographs graphically illustrate how the old course of the river still forms the foundations to the modern Shoreham Port.

Far left: The two turning basins can clearly be seen on the south side of the canal. *SPA*

Left: Sea water is a completely different colour to the water in the canal. On the left a cargo ship at Penney's Wharf and on the right Outer Lay-By Wharf. Beyond Lady Bee Marina on the north side of the canal is the bank that collapsed in 1957. *SPA*

Map of Shoreham port

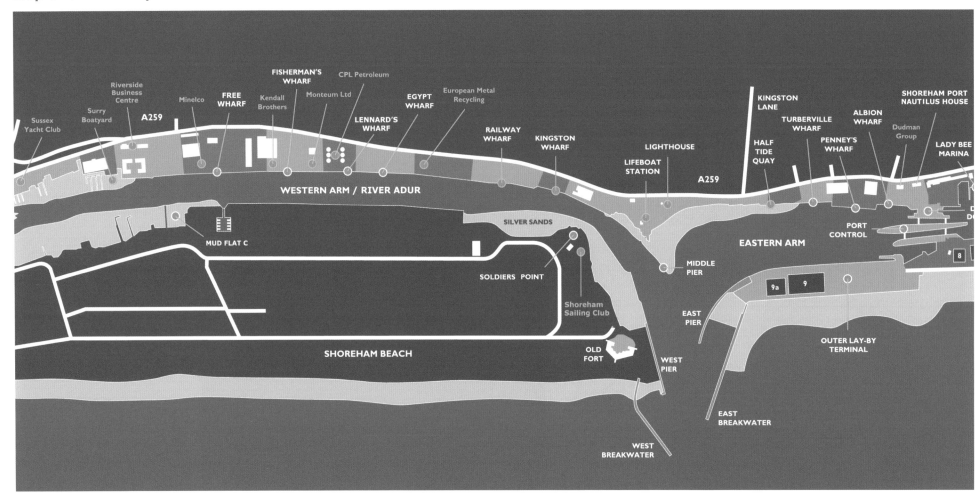

Sussex Yacht Club

Surry Boatyard

Riverside Business Centre

A259

Minelco

FREE WHARF

Kendall Brothers

FISHERMAN'S WHARF

Monteum Ltd

CPL Petroleum

LENNARD'S WHARF

EGYPT WHARF

European Metal Recycling

RAILWAY WHARF

KINGSTON WHARF

LIGHTHOUSE

LIFEBOAT STATION

A259

KINGSTON LANE

HALF TIDE QUAY

TURBERVILLE WHARF

PENNEY'S WHARF

ALBION WHARF

SHOREHAM PORT NAUTILUS HOUSE

Dudman Group

LADY BEE MARINA

WESTERN ARM / RIVER ADUR

MUD FLAT C

SILVER SANDS

SOLDIERS POINT

Shoreham Sailing Club

EASTERN ARM

PORT CONTROL

MIDDLE PIER

EAST PIER

8

9a

9

SHOREHAM BEACH

OLD FORT

WEST PIER

OUTER LAY-BY TERMINAL

EAST BREAKWATER

WEST BREAKWATER

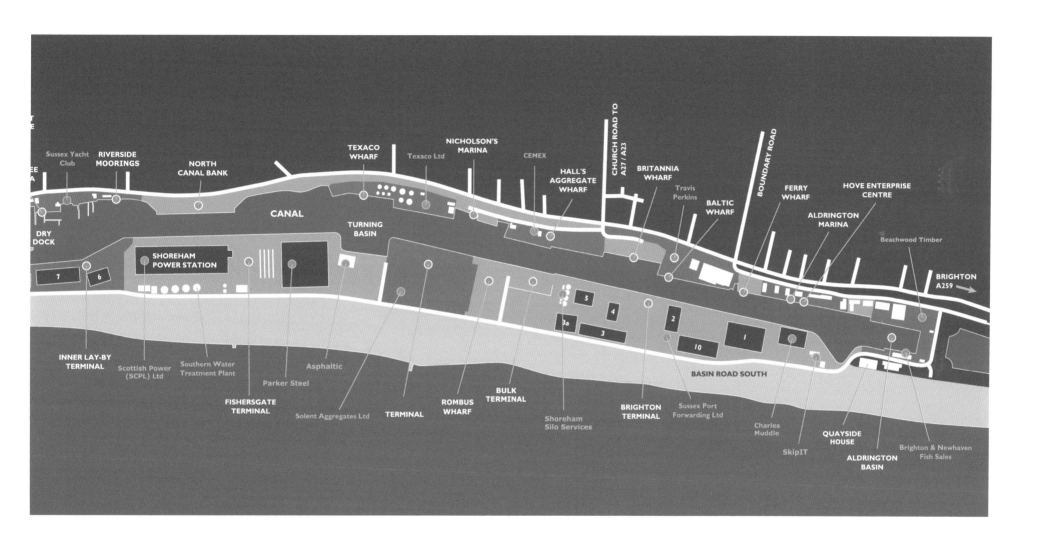

Sussex Yacht Club

RIVERSIDE MOORINGS

NORTH CANAL BANK

TEXACO WHARF

Texaco Ltd

NICHOLSON'S MARINA

CEMEX

HALL'S AGGREGATE WHARF

CHURCH ROAD TO A27 / A23

BRITANNIA WHARF

Travis Perkins

BALTIC WHARF

BOUNDARY ROAD

FERRY WHARF

HOVE ENTERPRISE CENTRE

ALDRINGTON MARINA

Beachwood Timber

DRY DOCK

CANAL

TURNING BASIN

SHOREHAM POWER STATION

7

6

BRIGHTON A259 →

5

4

2

3a

3

10

1

INNER LAY-BY TERMINAL

Scottish Power (SCPL) Ltd

Southern Water Treatment Plant

Parker Steel

Asphaltic

BASIN ROAD SOUTH

FISHERSGATE TERMINAL

Solent Aggregates Ltd

TERMINAL

ROMBUS WHARF

BULK TERMINAL

Shoreham Silo Services

BRIGHTON TERMINAL

Sussex Port Forwarding Ltd

Charles Muddle

SkipIT

QUAYSIDE HOUSE

ALDRINGTON BASIN

Brighton & Newhaven Fish Sales

James Kinnear, 'Southwick Harbour View', 1879. This picture looks west past the Schooner Inn and towards the lock. The south gut can be seen to the left and timber ponds in the foreground.
RP&M

Acknowledgements

Many people have given unsparingly of their time, expertise and enthusiasm in helping to make this book.

The project is the result of an idea of Dennis Scard, Chairman of Shoreham Port. Rod Johnstone, then Chief Executive of Shoreham Port, supported Dennis's idea. Subsequently Dennis and Rodney Lunn, the current Chief Executive of Shoreham Port, have had the energy and commitment to see the project to a conclusion. Within the port Keith Wadey has been an indispensible fount of knowledge: we always turned to him when in doubt or with a question to ask. Among various services, he helped find many of the illustrations in the port's archives, provided photographs of his own and commented on the text. Grateful thanks are also owed to Brian Blundell, Chris Bunby and Mary Hill.

Beyond the port special appreciation is due to Ken Wilcox who wrote the chapter 'The Pilots', lent photographs and provided immensely valuable comments on text and picture captions. Our thanks to Nigel Divers of the Southwick Society both for illustrations and his insightful comments on the text; James Thatcher of Marlipins Museum; Duncan McNeill from the Regency Society; and, St Julian's Church, Kingston Buci.

The editor expresses his sincere gratitude to Adam Trimingham, who researched and wrote the text, Jackie Marsh-Hobbs, the picture researcher who also wrote the captions to the illustrations, and Margot Richardson, the book's designer.

The authors, editor and the publisher wish to express their grateful thanks to the following for illustrative material and/or permission to reproduce it. Every effort has been made to trace and acknowledge holders of copyright of the illustrations used in this book, and the publishers would be pleased to hear from copyright holders concerning any errors or omissions.

DR: David Robinson
FG: Fred Gray
JGC: James Gray Collection/The Regency Society
JL: John Lucking
KenW: Ken Wilcox
KW: Keith Wadey
MM: Marlipins Museum, Sussex Archaeological Society
ND: from the collection of Nigel Divers
PM: Peter Marsh
RNLI: RNLI/John Periam
RP&M: Royal Pavilion & Museums Brighton & Hove
SBIT: Step Back In Time, 125 Queens Road, Brighton
SH: Shoreham Herald
SPA: Shoreham Port Authority
TNA: The National Archive ref DS 234/2 & ADM1 /15299
US: University of Sussex
WSRO: West Sussex Records Office

Bibliography

Graham Abbott, 'Shoreham Harbour's Rising Trade', *The Sussex County Magazine*, January, 1954

Cuttings from *The Argus* on Shoreham Port, 1955-1995

David Beevers, (ed) *Brighton Revealed Through Artists' Eyes c.1760 – c.1960* (Brighton, 1995)

H C Brookfield, 'A Critical Period in the History of Shoreham Harbour 1760 – 1816', *Sussex Archaeological Collections*, 88, 1949

Chris Butler, *West Sussex under Attack: Anti Invasion Sites 1500-1990* (Stroud, 2007)

Central Electricity Generating Board, *Brighton A Power Station: A Souvenir* (1976)

Central Electricity Generating Board, *Brighton and the Electrical Revolution 1882–1982* (1982)

Henry Cheal, *The Story of Shoreham* (Hove, 1921)

Nigel F Divers, *Southwick Remembered – The Story of Albion Street* (Southwick, 1996)

John H Farrant 'The Seaborne Trade of Sussex, 1720-1845', *Sussex Archaeological Collections*, 114, 1976

John H Farrant, 'The Rise and Decline of a South Coast Seafaring Town: Brighton 1550 – 1750', *The Mariners Mirror*, 71, 1, 1985

David Harries, *Maritime Sussex* (Seaford, 1997)

W A (Ted) Heasman, *Memories of Southwick and Kingston Buci* (Southwick, 2009)

T P Hudson (ed) 'Old and New Shoreham: Economic History', *A History of the County of Sussex*, 6, 1 (London, 1980)

Peter Longstaff-Tyrrell, *Front Line Sussex* (Stroud, 2000)

Frank R Mackley, *The First Eighty Years* (Henfield, 2007)

S P B Mais, *Sussex* (London, 1929)

Judy Middleton, *The Development of Shoreham Harbour, 1760 – 1880* (1984)

Judy Middleton, *The Encyclopaedia of Hove and Portslade* (Hove, 2002)

A Norton, *Project on Shoreham Harbour* (1970)

Richard Ollard, *The Escape of Charles II after the Battle of Worcester* (London, 1966)

Doris Randall, *A Southwick Century* (Southwick, 1999)

E Findlay Smith, 'Southwick Sketchbook', *Yachting Monthly*, 1919

Shoreham & District Historical Society, *Memories of Shoreham* (1994)

Shoreham Port Authority, Minutes and other records

Southwick Urban District Official Guide, 1969

Kenneth Wilcox, *Quaker Shipowning in the Port of Shoreham c. 1824 – 1880* (Greenwich, 2003)